Death and the Machine

Siobhan Lyons

Death and the Machine

Intersections of Mortality and Robotics

Siobhan Lyons
Department of Media, Music,
  Communication and Cultural
  Studies
Macquarie University
North Ryde, NSW, Australia

ISBN 978-981-13-0334-0   ISBN 978-981-13-0335-7   (eBook)
https://doi.org/10.1007/978-981-13-0335-7

Library of Congress Control Number: 2018939741

Cover illustration: © nemesis2207/Fotolia.co.uk

Printed on acid-free paper

This Palgrave Pivot imprint is published by the registered company Springer Nature
Singapore Pte Ltd. part of Springer Nature
The registered company address is: 152 Beach Road, #21-01/04 Gateway East, Singapore
189721, Singapore

ACKNOWLEDGEMENTS

This work has been completed with the generous time and support of a number of people. I would first like to thank Joshua Pitt for his unending support and guidance in the production of this book, and for giving me the opportunity to further my work in this field. I also wish to thank Sophie Li, for her assistance in editing and publishing the book. Thank you also to the other editors and reviewers at Palgrave and Springer whose rigorous and in-depth analysis and reviews of the book helped make it stronger. I would also like to thank John Potts and Ian Collinson for their helpful advice. And as always, my sincere gratitude must go to my parents, Fran and Patrick, for their ongoing support (intellectual, emotional, financial, etc.), without which none of my work would come to fruition.

CONTENTS

CHAPTER 1

Introduction: Can Robots Die?

Abstract This chapter introduces the key themes and questions that this book seeks to investigate. The question of whether or not a robot can be understood as a living *and dying* organism—technically, scientifically, biologically or philosophically—is introduced. I also discuss the origins of the term 'robot', and how this informs contemporary debates around the ethics of robots in the future.

Keywords Robots · Death · Media · Science · Humanity

Can robots die? This is the fundamental question that grounds and informs the basis of this book. Logically and presumably, a robot, or any 'non-human', cannot die, because it was never considered alive in the biological sense of the term to begin with. Seemingly, only that which organically lived can legitimately die: humans, animals, insects and other living organisms. Both biology and mortality determine a sense of *being*.

Death is assumed to be a universal phenomenon. Yet evidently, relationships between humans and animals, humans and other living organisms and humans and technology favour a particular hierarchy in which the human death is prioritised and valued. So what, then, of non-humans, those which increasingly populate society: the robots, replicants and other examples of artificial intelligence? Are these non-humans capable, in any way, of undergoing a certain demise, however non-biological? What validates a human's or non-human's claim

© The Author(s) 2018
S. Lyons, *Death and the Machine*,
https://doi.org/10.1007/978-981-13-0335-7_1

to die? How do we understand *natural* death with respect to *artificial* intelligence? Certainly, biology has factored greatly in the phenomenon of both life and death, with biological and scientific theory determining, to a large extent, the validity of one's existence and claim to life.

But in *Future Robots* (2014), Domenico Parisi argues against the manner in which science has claimed sovereignty over both the human and the machine in this respect. While psychology developed what it claimed to be a science of the mind, Parisi argues that 'science does not need only objective and quantitative data. It also needs theories that explain the data. The problem with psychology is that while its empirical methods are those of science, its theoretical vocabulary is still a philosophical vocabulary' (2014: 4). This is why, he argues, a psychology of human behaviour is only a 'half-science' (3).

But science has become the benchmark from which all phenomena are measured, which has led not to greater security and faith in objectivity, but a decline in imagination. As Adorno and Horkheimer famously noted in *Dialectic of Enlightenment* (1944), the enlightenment sought to liberate society by way of scientific objectivity, succeeding only in imprisoning people in unquestionable rationality, devoid of imagination, creativity and possibility. They write: 'On their way towards modern science human beings have discarded meaning. The concept is replaced by the formula, the cause by rules and probability' (2002: 3). They also observe that 'science itself has no awareness of itself; it is merely a tool. Enlightenment, however, is the philosophy which equates truth with the scientific system' (66). This 'bourgeois philosophy', in their estimation, produced a system in which 'freedom in their world tended towards organised anarchy', in which 'pure reason became unreason, a procedure as immune to errors as it was devoid of content' (71).

Daniel Dennett, too, emphasises the imagination in conjunction with scientific theory in his work *Consciousness Explained* (1991). For Dennett, the discoveries of neuroscience are not enough (1993: 16), and the imagination becomes crucial in exploring ways in which machines could live (which explains the tremendous sway and importance of popular culture's role in constantly re-examining the robot's existence). In this respect, within this book I adopt a relativistic approach, primarily relying upon analogical thinking to examine the status of the human in a world increasingly transfixed by the gradual emergence of artificial intelligence, and what such an emergence challenges about assumed notions of existence and, ultimately, of death.

Indeed, as culture and technology increasingly converge with the advent of humanoid robots, one must reconsider the boundaries of existence and death where artificial life is concerned. In previous years, popular culture has been primarily concerned with the question of life regarding artificial intelligence. This book, however, focuses on the question of death regarding robots and other non-humans, since death and mortality, greatly influence notions of humanity and being.

But to examine what it means to die, one must first re-examine what it means to be alive, or what constitutes an 'authentic' human, before considering what it means to experience an 'authentic' death. Discussions regarding death and robotics almost uniformly frame this curious dynamic negatively, positioning robots as adversaries and the cause of many human deaths. With the first death of a human as a result of a robot occurring in 1979, and the most recent occurring in 2015, discussions surrounding the ambiguous nature of responsibility in robotics and machinery have proliferated, with the question of robot accountability being situated at the forefront of media discourse.

However, rarely, if ever, does critical discussion navigate the ethical considerations and potential of a 'robot death', as it appears fundamentally contradictory. How can that which never fulfilled the parameters of living existence be deemed validly dead? How can artificial life undergo or experience a natural death? And if we permit such an idea, what implications does this pose for biological humanity as we understand it?

Despite such apparent contradictions, however, discussion regarding the mortal capacity of a robot has increasingly graced media reportage; in January 2017, it was reported that monkeys featured in a documentary on BBC's *Spy in the Wild* were mourning over the 'death' of a baby monkey robot,[1] which had been used to spy on them. During filming, the robot was accidentally crushed. Media commentary had reported that the robot had 'died', based on the fact that the other, living monkeys, were mourning it. As well as this, reportage on the robots that had been sent into Fukushima in 2016 noted that the robots had 'died' due to radiation poisoning that had caused their systems to malfunction and shut down.

---

[1] See Toby Meyjes, 'Distraught monkeys mourn death of robotic monkey spying on them', *Metro*, 11 January 2017, http://metro.co.uk/2017/01/11/distraught-monkeys-mourn-death-of-robotic-monkey-spying-on-them-6375436/ (accessed 26 July 2017).

The language in such reporting is particularly significant, as the robots are said to have 'died', rather than having been destroyed, or shut down. These are the first instances of robots being discussed in the media in actual biological terms; they had actually 'died', suggesting, then, that attitudes towards the mortal capacity of robots is changing, however moderately.

Society has long discussed the extent to which a robot may be considered human, and questioned whether or not such a being is capable of achieving sentience; the 2016 release of the television series *Westworld*—based on the 1973 film of the same name—is testament to the continued curiosity in robots and their potential for consciousness. The interest in the topic of robots attaining consciousness stems from its implications for humanity as a whole; if a robot may be permitted the title of 'human', then previously stable definitions of humanity become obsolete or, at the very least, unstable, which threatens the very fabric of our existence on ontological terms. This prompts certain questions about why we would ever want to ascribe or permit 'life' for non-human machines.

Timothy Morton discusses the need to develop solidarity with non-humans in his work *Humankind* (2017), saying that 'difficulties of solidarity between humans' are in fact 'repressing and suppressing possibilities of solidarity with non-humans' (15). For Morton, 'Human worlds are not different in value from non-human ones' (14). He also posits that 'non-sentient non-human life forms (as far as we know) and non-life (and also by implication the non-sentient and non-living parts of humans) also have worlds' (14). These worlds, however ambiguous or esoteric they may be, are in some way existent.

Of course, as Thomas Nagel famously noted in his paper 'What is it like to be a Bat?' (1974), certain kinds of experiences of being are beyond the capacity and grasp of human consciousness and understanding. This means that we cannot know what it is to be a bat, no matter how sophisticated our technology becomes or how our own internal consciousness may change. A human cannot think outside of their own cultural existence, outside of culture. We may imagine what it is to be a bat, but can never experience what it *is* to be a bat. Likewise, while we cannot imagine what it is for a robot to live, this does not negate or invalidate the notion that a machine has its own world of value. While Nagel argues that 'an organism has conscious mental states if and only if there is something that it is like to be that organism—something that it is like for the organism to be itself', Morton's argument suggests that a robot may have a way of feeling like a robot, and therefore may validate the notion of machine consciousness.

But while we have become fascinated by the question of what might make a robot a living being capable of its own experience, we have neglected the role that death plays in such circumstances. Since death is understood as one of the most important factors determining the validity of humanity, it seems necessary to examine whether the robot and other machines can achieve the very element that determines the human life, and what this means for humanity if it ever *could* be achieved. Beyond the human's mere appearance or behaviour, death fundamentally determines the validity of life, as seen in *The Bicentennial Man*, in which the robot, Andrew Martin, is not deemed human because he is immortal. As Anders and Krell note, 'in this story, the cost of being recognized as human is mortality' (2013).

Death, of course, is instinctively understood as a biological phenomenon, just like consciousness. But this work will discuss the notion that death may exceed biology and also be technological in nature, or at least the idea of death may expand to the technological realm. By reframing either the parameters of humanity or the parameters of death, the robot death may come to be embraced as a significant phenomenon in contemporary, post-human culture.

Throughout this work, books and films from across science fiction and popular culture will be used to discuss and speculate on the nature of a robot's or other non-human's mortal capacity. Popular culture is useful, moreover imperative, in serving as a speculative tool to examine the ethical potential of artificial intelligence. While robots and other humanoids in everyday life have not yet achieved the kind of consciousness or personality familiar to popular works such as Isaac Asimov's *I, Robot* or *Westworld* (and possibly never will), their existence serves to enlighten us on the topic and parameters of humanity. We may better understand the nature of humanity by looking at that which seeks to be human, specifically through the lens of death, the ultimate factor in determining humanity.

The actual word 'robot' was first coined in 1920 by Czech writer Karel Čapek (though a letter from Čapek to his brother, Josef, suggests that his brother actually invented the word). The word appeared in Čapek's science fiction play *Rossum's Universal Robots* (*R.U.R.*). In the play, man-made roboti, or robots, who resemble human beings, are manufactured at a factory and are expected to work for humans, before a robot rebellion occurs that wipes out the human race.

The term 'robot' originates from the Czech word 'robota', meaning 'slave' or 'serf labour', and denotes a form of hard work. Thus the very term robot has its origins in labour, a persevering trope in society that, ironically, has led to a corresponding anxiety regarding work opportunities for humans in a culture dominated by robotic labour.[2] But as Andrew Charlton and Jim Chalmers point out, automation is not new, and human jobs have been compromised severely since the Industrial Revolution, but despite this, mass unemployment has not occurred: 'it seems the gloomy soothsayers didn't overestimate the capability of machine; they underestimated human capacity to change existing jobs and create new ones' (2017).

Alongside the implications of increased automation, robot ethics is an emerging discourse in science and technology, which is predominantly concerned with the moral issues surrounding the responsibility of a robot in life or death situations, such as warfare or personal assistance to the infirm. In 2017, two crucial developments in the area of robotics and AI attested to the divergent approaches to the future of robots. While Elon Musk and other robot experts signed a letter to the United Nations to put a ban on autonomous weaponry or 'killer robots', a Beneficial AI conference was held in January, 2017 in Asilomar, California.

What we see here is the separation of robotics into two distinct but related spheres of thought and anticipation: on the one hand there is the group that fears a robot takeover—whether in the form of labour or from a threat to assumed human superiority—and seeks to ameliorate this threat by taking affirmative action against the implementation of more robots. On the other hand, there is the group that sees the increased use of robots as potentially beneficial. Certainly the advent of the Internet of Things (IoT) with developments such as Amazon Echo illustrate that people's attitudes towards having this technology in the home as another family member shows a modest willingness to *humanise* that technology.

In any case, the proliferation of discussions surrounding the place of the robot in societies in the future provoke questions not about the future of robotics, but the future of humanity, and ultimately what effect the robot's place in society will have on the very notion of humanity.

---

[2] See Dan Shewan, 'Robots will destroy our jobs—and we're not ready for it', *The Guardian* (11 January 2017), https://www.theguardian.com/technology/2017/jan/11/robots-jobs-employees-artificial-intelligence (accessed 23 July 2017).

As James Canton notes in his book *Future Smart* (2015), changes in technology ultimately suggest that artificial intelligence and the human brain may merge to create artificial consciousness or 'synthetic minds'. This evidently provokes a number of ethical and practical concerns, many of which will be discussed in the following chapters.

The second chapter of this book provide a discussion on various approaches to the phenomenon of death; looking at a number of philosophers including Epicurus and Freud, this chapter shows that although it acts as the ultimate validation of humanity, the phenomenon of death itself is currently in the process of a radical shift in the sciences and humanities. The development of technologies in the sciences have provoked questions regarding the ability for a human to delay death and prolong their lives, which shows, among other things, another changing facet in the history and future of 'stable humanities'. In this chapter, I also discuss the continued fear and avoidance of death that defines and validates humanity, while also providing examples of the way in which 'death' is already in the process of being reconsidered.

The third chapter will delve into ethical debates surrounding the proposition of a machine consciousness. Before looking at the notion of a robot death, in this chapter I explore the phenomenon of a 'robot life'. Questions surrounding the adequate development of biological consciousness, and how this intrudes upon ideas of machine consciousness, are discussed, showing that while machine consciousness is currently hypothetical, the proposals of such a development will invariably alter previous, 'stable' definitions of humanity. The second chapter will also look further into the fear that society holds for humans amidst increasingly sophisticated robotics, using Masahiro Mori's theory of the 'uncanny valley' to explain society's continued discomfort regarding robots.

In the fourth chapter of this book, I examine the way in which the robot death has been theorised and hypothesised in popular culture, looking at films and shows such as *Blade Runner, 2001: A Space Odyssey*, and *Westworld* to inform a discussion on the ontology of humanity and robotics in regards to death. As Martha Nussbaum has articulated in *Love's Knowledge* (1990), fiction is particularly useful in such ethical discussions as it improves our ability to recognise broader moral and ethical issues and increases our understanding of certain complex ethical structures within society. She argues that literature and art help to explore 'important questions about human beings and human life' (1992: 5). We can extend this to argue that literature, art and the media more broadly can help us ask important questions about the potential for robot life by granting the imagination its rightly dues. Looking at the specific semantics that are used in popular culture for various 'non-humans', such as robots, replicants and clones, I show not only that death is not considered a universal phenomenon, but that behaviour, rather than biology, can be used as a potential determining factor in the structure of the 'ideal' human.

Such arguments are, indeed, relative and hypothetical. And yet these arguments serve to challenge certain privileged assumptions regarding the place and existence of the human in society. Humanity has long benefited from an assumed link between biology and consciousness, a link that, due to progressing science and technology, is being questioned and challenged. As technology becomes increasingly sophisticated to the point that we can actually somehow produce synthetic minds, it becomes overwhelmingly necessary to then examine the ethical, philosophical and practical impacts that this will have on assumed notions of what it means to be human.

<h1 style="text-align:center">REFERENCES</h1>

Adorno, Theodor, and Horkheimer, Max. *Dialectic of Enlightenment: Philosophical Fragments*. Stanford: Stanford University Press, 2002.

Anders, Charlie Jane, and Krell, Jason. '10 Robot Deaths That Were More Moving Than Almost Any Human's'. *Gizmodo*. December 6, 2013. Retrieved November 13, 2017, from https://io9.gizmodo.com/10-robot-deaths-that-were-more-moving-than-almost-any-h-1477252355.

Canton, James. *Future Smart: Managing the Game-Changing Trends That Will Transform Your World*. Boston: Da Capo Press, 2015.

Charlton, Andrew, and Chalmers, Jim. 'The Robot Race: What Does Automation Mean for the Future of Jobs?' *The Monthly*. November 2017. Retrieved January 12, 2018, from https://www.themonthly.com.au/issue/2017/november/1509454800/andrew-charlton-and-jim-chalmers/robot-race.

Dennett, Daniel. *Consciousness Explained*. London: Penguin, 1993.

Morton, Timothy. *Humankind: Solidarity with Nonhuman People*. London: Verso, 2017.

Nagel, Thomas. 'What Is It to Be a Bat?' *The Philosophical Review*. Vol. 83, No. 4, October 1974, pp. 435–450.

Nussbaum, Martha. *Love's Knowledge: Essays on Philosophy and Literature*. New York: Oxford University Press, 1992.

Parisi, Domenico. *Future Robots: Towards a Robotic Science of Human Beings*. Advances in Interaction Studies. Volume 7. Amsterdam and Philadelphia: John Benjamins, 2014.

CHAPTER 2

Death, Humanity and Existence

Abstract In this chapter, I discuss the significance of death in regards to understanding humanity and existence. I examine how the fear of death is seen to define humanity, and is often understood as a uniquely biological phenomenon. This chapter also discusses the development of transhumanism, with robots becoming more human-like, and humans becoming more machine-like in their quest for immortality. Such developments are radically altering the conventional understanding of what it means to be a human and what it means to die. While the parameters of humanity are being amended to potentially include machines, the notion of death itself is also being reconfigured to potentially accommodate a non-biological death.

Keywords Death · Robots · Biology · Immortality · Transhumanism

Death fundamentally determines our existence as human beings. Essentially, that which dies is granted significance through the temporariness of being. Yet the act of evading, surpassing or obliterating death has continually occupied a significant place in both popular culture and scientific circles. But in our efforts to erase, overcome, or conquer death, previous discourses that circulated around the link between death and humanity, therefore, are subject to change. Science and technology allow us to consider the possibility that we can alleviate the threat of death, and in so doing, we inadvertently manipulate the parameters of humanity, removing the human further from the phenomenon of death, and correspondingly allowing other so-called 'non-human' beings to operate closer to it. The relationship between death and existence is particularly significant in the age of artificial intelligence; if we typically understand death as equating ideas of what it means to be human, then immortal AI do not fit this profile. Science fiction and general discourse usually circulates around this assumption. Yet in attempting to surpass death, humans are unwittingly implying that non-biological beings, specifically machines, may too be able to be considered human, for those for whom death no longer sustains the definition of humanity. Such discussions have also threatened the ability to which death can any longer define us as humans.

Human beings have long had an ambiguous, if not tempestuous relationship with their mortality. Yet the notion that death fundamentally determines humanity is one that continues to hold sway, advances in technology notwithstanding. David Goldman argues, in fact, that an 'awareness of death defines the human condition, so that human beings cannot bear their own mortality without the hope of immortality' (2011: xix). But while immortality and the extension of humankind's lifespan is gaining increasing traction in science and technology, more philosophical discussions regarding death revolve around its implications for the human and the meaning of life.

In Cozzolino and Blackie's chapter 'I die, therefore I am', they share Goldman's assertion of humanity depending on an *awareness* of death, observing that while death is a daunting prospect, 'death awareness enables or facilitates a focus on the time we do have and as a result can fuel our desires to find meaning [in life]' (2013: 33). In this way, a machine cannot be considered in any way human or living, not because they are unable to die, but because they lack an awareness of death and their own sense of non-being. Hence death awareness is considered a fundamentally human trait.

Cozzolino and Blackie distinguish between those who actively avoid considering the notion of death out of fear, and those that engage with its realities in secular ways through embracing values such as altruism and creativity. They note that while 'few people yearn for death' (41), 'confronting death head-on generates a recalibration of the self' (42). For Cozzolino and Blackie, 'a specific and individuated awareness of mortality seems to enable a reawakening of the specific-self, which facilitates authentic and intrinsic pursuits of meaning'. In contrast, those for whom death purposefully remains an abstract concept struggle to attain sufficient meaning in life. As they put it, 'the best description of death is "the absence of life", but in our view "the absence of death" utterly fails to capture the richness of living. Viewed in this manner, life is the real mystery, not death' (42).

Death has never been too far from the cultural radar in each generation, though it seemed to be of less interest in the early nineteenth and early to mid-twentieth century, prompting Joseph Jacobs to quip in 1899 that 'death is no longer in fashion' (1899) (a response in the *Spectator* called this 'untenable', arguing that 'death must always remain the most striking and, therefore the most keenly noted, fact in life' (1899: 180). But Howarth and Leaman argue that 'despite two world wars yielding death on an industrial scale, the increasing reluctance in many societies to discuss mortality appeared to be a feature of twentieth-century living' (2001: xv).

However, by the late 1990s, death seemed to re-emerge as a subject of philosophical, social and scientific interest, with television shows such as *Buffy the Vampire Slayer, Twin Peaks, The Sopranos* and even *Seinfeld* frequently exploring the topic. And with the development of artificial intelligence and the sophistication of new technologies, the question of death and its place in the life of a human has resurfaced with increasing resonance in twenty-first century culture. Indeed, for Howarth and Leaman, by the twenty-first century, dying and death 'has become the source of culture and pertinent to the fabric of life' (xv). According to Cooter (2003), 'this explosion of interest in death reflects the belief amongst biologists that the mystery of life has been solved through its reduction to DNA' (479).

But this reliance on scientific explanation is only partly reliable, and DNA is only one element that attempts to explain the significance and meaning of life and death. For as Adorno and Horkheimer noted, science can only take us so far in understanding these concepts. Philosophy has remained significant in its insights into death.

Deleuze and Guattari speculate on the notion of death as an incessant experience in every moment of life:

> The experience of death is the most common of occurrences in the unconscious, precisely because it occurs in life and for life, in every passage or becoming, in every intensity as passage or becoming [...] death is what is felt in every feeling, what never ceases and never finishes happening in

every becoming—in the becoming-another-sex, the becoming-god, the
becoming-a-race, etc., forming zones of intensity on the body without
organs. Every intensity controls within its own life the experience of death
and envelops it. (2004: 363)

Despite the fact that animals and other living organisms experience
death, it is humans that are more intimately acquainted with death,
since humans seem to be one of the only living beings that are aware of
their own eventual or imminent demise. What is more, human beings
resume their lives in spite of this awareness of their own mortality. As
Plinio Prioresch argues, 'it is one of the truly remarkable facts of life that
man, while realising that death is inevitable, continues to pursue the
day-to-day routine of existence' (1990: 43).

The notion of death being specifically available to humans produces
a value system that prioritises the human. As Martin Heidegger argued,
'mortals are they who can experience death *as* death' (1982: 107), highlighting a distinction between humans and other beings. The assumption
here is that only that which is mortal can experience a legitimate death,
forbidding all non-humans the same luxury. Animals, for example, are
another being that Heidegger separates from humans in terms of death.
In this way, while the animal does die, for Heidegger it similarly lacks the
emotional significance of a human death. The machine becomes another
non-human being that is deprived of the characteristic of death, since
they are first and foremost deprived of the characteristic of life.

But the current preoccupation with artificial intelligence has sparked a
number of questions about the future state of humans and machines. As
humans become more technological in appearance, possessing artificial
limbs and implants, robots are becoming more humanlike. Beyond mere
appearance, moreover, the stable boundaries that have continually separated humans and machines are dissolving, allowing for a new approach
to conventional understanding regarding the human's prioritised place in
life and death.

FEAR OF DEATH

In his Pulitzer Prize-winning work *The Denial of Death* (1973), Ernest
Becker persuasively argues that 'of all things that move man, one of the
principal ones is his terror of death' (11). There has been, he argues, a
significant amount of interest and research into the fear or avoidance

of death in anthropological, scientific and philosophical circles, noting, in contrast to Howarth and Leavon, that there was a revival of interest in the concept of death in the twentieth century. Speaking from a psychoanalytic perspective, Becker's position is that we suppress the fear of death and the anxiety of mortality. He writes, 'after Darwin the problem of death as an evolutionary one came to the fore, and many thinkers immediately saw that it was a major psychological problem' (11). Referring to theorist Gregory Zilboorg's views on the matter, Becker notes that rarely are we confronted with the immediacy of death in our everyday circumstances, which is why the fear of death is something that is underlying but not all-consuming. This is also what separates humans from animals somewhat, since the threat of death appears, if not constant in the animal kingdom, then certainly more predominant than in the life of a human being. Yet the threat remains for humans, Becker notes, revealing a particular paradox about our relationship to death: 'We can understand what seems like an impossible paradox: the ever-present fear of death in the normal biological functioning of our instinct of self-preservation, as well as our utter obliviousness to this fear in our conscious life' (17).

Hence Becker significantly aligns a fear of death with the 'normal biological functioning' of humanity. The human is biologically compelled, in many views, towards self-preservation. This is something that cannot necessarily be programmed into a machine; the fear of death is linked to a primal, biological instinct and is therefore not 'mechanical' in nature.

Indeed, the fear of death is perhaps the most natural feeling amongst humans. Beyond mere biological necessity, in which a fear of death keeps us alive, fear of the unknown drives much of the distrust or fear of death. As well as this, the mere pleasure that many people experience in simply being alive determines the threat of death as a state of *non-being*. For John Fischer, there is an important distinction between dying, death and being dead: 'dying is a process. Being dead is a condition or state. Death intervenes between dying and being dead' (1993: 3–4). But the precise moment when death intervenes is more ambiguous. Indeed, 'the definition of the precise point at which a living organism ceases to live belongs to those problems that seem easy at first sight but turn out to be very complicated when further analysed' (Prioresch 1990: 49).

The mystery surrounding the precise moment and nature of death informs many of the debates regarding a robot's inability to die; not only does a robot not possess the kind of 'life' that humans reserve for living organisms, but the state at which it can be considered 'dead' remains ambiguous. We use uniquely human terms to describe computers: they can 'sleep', 'hibernate', but they can also 'shut down'. We control a computer's ability to turn back on, but once a machine breaks down irreparably, it is considered 'dead'. But this state of inanimateness does not illicit genuine grief in us, at least, not at all in the same way that a human's death does, because its state of death is mechanical. It is considered a 'non-death', because the machine is considered a non-living entity. A distinction is therefore made between human death and a machine death, belonging to a specific hierarchy. The absence of fear in a machine death, alongside a lack of biology, determines and sustains this hierarchy. Yet as Timothy Morton argues, 'the life-nonlife distinction is impossible to maintain; all beings are better thought as undead, not as animate or inanimate' (23).

Famously, for Epicurus, death is neither a bad thing and nor can it impact the human, since, for Epicurus, death is something *separate* from us, an event which cannot actually be experienced. Epicurus posits that we ought not to fear death therefore, because the dead person cannot experience fear, and the living person will not adequately *experience* death. While we may fear the process of *dying*, whether through pain or an awareness of an imminent death, the state of being dead alleviates the threat of fear.

Epicurus' thoughts notwithstanding, the fear of death has informed much of society's artistic and cultural work, and continues to define approaches to life and living. In contrast to the notion that death ought not to be feared, Fischer argues that death is bad 'primarily because it deprives the deceased of goods—the goods he would have enjoyed if he had lived' (326). While we can assume that most of these goods are material or physical—food, shelter, sex, warmth, books, etc. They also pertain to the mere enjoyment of *being*, of consciousness and thought. We enjoy being able to engage with certain pleasures, but we also simply enjoy *being*. And since death is a state of non-being, our fears about death are both unsurprising and understandable. But because a robot is understood as living in servitude, rather than living just for its own sake, death is not seen to be an important factor. For humans, the pleasure of being alive makes death an unpleasant fact.

For Russian Orthodox philosopher Nikolai Fedorov, death not only is the greatest enemy of humanity, but it also has no bearing on the existence of humanity in any ontological sense. In his work *What Was Man Created For?* (1990), he emphatically states that death is an enemy of humankind, and denies that it has any philosophical value, stating that it is 'not a quality which determines what a human being is and must be' (2008: 99). In fact, according to Stephen Lukashevich, Fedorov would only sleep for four or five hours a night, since he 'disliked the deathlike nature of sleep' (1977: 18).

Yet for the purposes of this book, death becomes, in fact, tremendously important in determining not only what a human being is, but what a human being *can be*. This avoidance of death, so characteristic of the human species, is similarly that which defines humanity. An avoidance or fear of death promotes the integrity of life, and the ability to die confers upon the living a particular significance that appears reserved for the human species. Machines are predominantly excluded from this discourse, but their increasing presence in society only reinforces the neglected importance of death in the overarching sequence of life.

Sigmund Freud was more open to the notion of death, calling it a 'necessary termination of life', and that 'every one of us owes nature his death and must be prepared to pay his debt, in short, that death was natural, undeniable, and inevitable' (2001: 289). Yet he also observed that 'we have shown an unmistakeable tendency to put death aside, to eliminate it from life'. Indeed, in recent years, as the possibility to extend life has emerged optimistically in the sciences, the radical prospect of eliminating death altogether has both captured the imagination of artists and alleviated the threat of mortality for the average human, for whom death has always been and would always be a given.

In *Being and Time*, Heidegger describes a process of 'being-towards-death', in which death is linked to a sense of authenticity, and is almost a liberating factor associated with time: 'The existential project of an authentic being-towards-death must thus set forth the factors of such a being, which are constitutive for it as an understanding of death—in the sense of being towards this possibility without fleeing it or covering it over' (2010: 250).

Like Freud, Heidegger emphasises a confrontation with death, rather than a denial or fleeing of it. He characterises it as a *'being towards a possibility*, towards an eminent possibility of Dasein [existence] itself' (250), as though to argue that death *constitutes* authenticity. As Simon Critchley more clearly articulates about the being-towards-death: 'if we want to understand what it means to be an authentic human being, then it is essential that we constantly project our lives onto the horizon of our death'.

Death is thus seen to validate and authenticate humanity, whether we avoid it or not, in such a way as to preclude other artificial beings. Since death is unavoidable, a fear of it seems to stem also from a lack of control. For Heidegger, as for Freud and Epicurus, it's not enough to fear or avoid death, but to incorporate it into our *being-in-the-world*: 'Brooding over death does not completely take away from it its character of possibility. It is always brooded over as something coming, but we weaken it by calculating how to have death under our control'. Instead, he argues that the being-towards-death, or our awareness of its relative immanence, 'must be understood *as possibility*, cultivated *as possibility* and *endured as possibility* in our relation to it'. In discussing the anticipation of being-towards-death, Heidegger's point is not that we are morbidly waiting for death, but rather that, as Critchley puts it, anticipation 'mobilises mortality as the condition for free action in the world'. Death therefore is a liberating force in this respect.

Hence, as with David Goldman, it is not merely death which epitomises the human condition, but our awareness of it, and our awareness and acceptance of it as a possibility producing an authentic human being.

Indeed, more so than death itself, it is our precise fear or awareness of it that seems to indicate our humanity, since fear is a primal, not mechanistic trait. Our ability to be aware and accept death is something intrinsically human; the inability to program a fear of death into a robot seems, at least at this stage in robotics, to invalidate the ability for a robot to ever be considered living. In order to be alive, there needs to be the threat of death, both in biological and psychological terms. While a robot may be switched off at some stage, or even become broken beyond repair, it does not have an awareness of what either process actually entails, even if we consider it a *kind* of death. Its 'death' is seen as illegitimate due to a lack of a corresponding awareness of itself and of its own state of non-functioning.

This is not to say, then, that a robot could never therefore be considered either a living or dying being. What this simply means is that, as with a state of living, a state of dying, for a robot, depends on a fundamental awareness of this process. Not only would a robot need to possess sentience, in a conscious sense, but so too would a robot be required to have some awareness of their *transience*. The philosophical paradox of being aware of our eventual demise seems to define and shape humanity more so than death itself, since a state of living is irretrievably linked to a state of several kinds of awareness, both of life *and* death.

TRANSHUMANISM AND THE CONQUEST OF DEATH

If Heidegger cautions against having complete control over death, or trying to flee it, his view is not readily embraced in a culture whose scientific achievements have corresponded to the possibility of extending life. As technology improves for possibilities of artificial intelligence, so too has the technology to prolong human life. Yet the current condition in relation to death is not as simple as striving for immortality; many scientific discussions circulate around the desire to *extend* one's lifespan, in the same way as the replicants in *Blade Runner*, as will be discussed in the fourth chapter. This desire to extend life seems in and of itself fundamentally human through its sense of desperation.

Ironically, in the case of robotics and death, humanity often strives for *immortality* through advancing technologies and sciences, while robots appear, in popular culture, to strive for the validation of humanity through *mortality*. Due to humankind's well-known fear of death, we often discuss the scientific conquest of our own mortality, despite mortality operating as the defining characteristic of humanity. In this manner, humans may be becoming less human in a biological, post-human context, while robots and other non-humans appear to be attaining greater humanly characteristics through a desire for consciousness. And since one of the defining characteristics of humanity is death, then the robot's desire for a biological death would seem to suitably validate their categorisation of 'human', more so than other characteristics such as their appearance or their mechanical structure.

Definitions regarding both death and humanity are changing; death no longer commands the finality it once did, directly impacting our understanding of the human. The dual phenomena of the post-human life, or *transhumanism*, imply a radical break with previous notions of existence and mortality. There is possibly no coincidence between the threat of climate change, discussions regarding the sixth extinction and humanity's interest in extending their own lifespan. As Claire Colebrook explains, '"We" late near-extinction humans appear to be addicted to witnessing annihilation, to the feeling of near-death or posthuman existence' (2014: 91). In this manner, what we are seeing is not necessarily the twilight of the human species in geological history, but, perhaps, a fundamental transition in what *constitutes* a human being as machine and human increasingly merge. Humans already rely on machine technology to such an extent—through artificial limbs and organs—that what constituted a human half a century ago is in a state of flux. But there is no known ratio between flesh and machine that exists to determine one's status as either human or machine. When does the human end and the machine begin?

Emerging discourses in anthropocentrism shed crucial light on the fate of humanity in a finite world. As Roy Scranton notes in his work *Learning to Die in the Anthropocene*:

> For humanity to survive in the Anthropocene, we need to learn to live with and through the end of our current civilization. Change, risk, conflict, strife, and death are the very processes of life, and we cannot avoid them. We must learn to accept and adapt. The human psyche naturally rebels against the idea of its end. Likewise, civilizations have throughout history marched blindly toward disaster, because humans are wired to believe that tomorrow will be much like today. (22)

This fear of collective annihilation is not merely based on death alone; it is human obsoleteness that defines much of this pattern. Facing what Elizabeth Kolbert calls the Sixth Extinction (2014), alongside what Scranton states is the fact that 'this civilisation is already dead' (23), humans are naturally inclined to see death as more than just a personal fate, but something that translates into eventual, collective obscurity. Such a reality terrifies us more than any kind of personal injury. As Genevieve Bell writes, the ongoing fear of a robot invasion has more to do with the threat of becoming irrelevant. Films such as *Her* and *Ex Machina*, she explains, 'underline a particular set of concerns, which is not that the machines will kill us but that we will become irrelevant' (Tucker 2016). Bell notes that we have a fear that robots will eventually abandon us, as seen in the aforementioned films. Hence much of the fear that circulates around robotics relates more to sudden insignificance, rather than annihilation.

But the issue regarding humanity's relationship with robots goes even further than eventual obscurity. It's not only the thought that our machines will leave us that proves disconcerting, but that they will replace us as the next dominant species on earth once humans are gone, rendering us obsolete. So our efforts to challenge our mortality are not at all surprising in an anthropocentric context.

One of the most interesting and relevant works on humanity's efforts to defy death through science is *The Scientific Conquest of Death* (2004), compiled by the Immortality Institute, a non-for-profit company based in Houston, Texas. The company, like the book, encourages the extension of humankind's lifespan, and aims to reduce or eliminate the ageing process, while preventing those deaths that can potentially be prevented. Mike Treder, in his chapter 'Emancipation from Death', challenges the concept of that which is 'natural', noting: 'Tooth decay is natural – should dentistry be outlawed? [...] Cholera is natural – should we allow epidemics to rage unchallenged? Death is natural – must it continue to wreak its dreadful havoc?' (188–189). He further states that 'if modern science and technology can safely improve the human condition by overcoming natural limits, including ageing and death, then they should be used to this end' (189).

In addition to living without death, Treder argues, one manner in which to extend the life of humans is to upload our personalities into 'a virtually indestructible robot' (190), since our bodies, he writes, are 'unacceptably ephemeral' (191). This is the very plot of the 2014 film *Transcendence*, in which Dr. Will Caster (Johnny Depp) has his consciousness uploaded to a computer. As discussed in the next chapter, the merging of technology and consciousness in this way is gaining traction in the scientific industry. Indeed, if humanity is more about consciousness than it is about our bodies, than the act of uploading consciousness into a computer seems to be something of a philosophically plausibility.

All of these assertions seem to imply an end to death, but the irony in these developments in light of the debates regarding a robot's mortal capacity should be clearly apparent; the desire to defy death, while not inherently surprising, is significant to the extent that it implies the drastic removal of one of the crucial factors that seem to determine our humanity. And this stalwart defiance of death manifesting itself through the (currently far-fetched) prospect of uploading ourselves into a machine seems to suggest that we actually envy robots and the machine. While rebuking robots for the threat (mortal or philosophical) that they pose to humanity, our films and speculative works suggest that we are quite content with using them to further our own lives. It is unsurprising then that the desire to extend ourselves beyond the limitations of biological humanity continues to dominate discussion in science and technology, focusing on the fate of the human in a technological culture.

For instance, Google engineer Ray Kurzweil stated in 2015 that humans will likely become hybrids by the year 2030, arguing that we will become a 'hybrid of biological and non-biological thinking' (Griffin 2015). He stresses the need to 'merge and enhance ourselves', stating that 'that's the nature of being human—we transcend out limitations'. Tesla and SpaceX founder Elon Musk, too, has advocated this post-human mergence between flesh and technology, claiming that humans ought to become cyborgs in order to avoid becoming inferior to vastly more intelligent robots: 'Under any rate of advancement in AI we will be left behind by a lot. The benign situation with ultra-intelligent AI is that we would be so far below in intelligence [that] we'd be like a pet, or a house cat' (Warren 2016).

There are already cyborgs currently in existence. Neil Harbisson, a colour-blind man from Northern Ireland, is the first person to be considered a cyborg after implanting an antenna into his skull, the operation of which was performed by an anonymous surgeon, since the medical profession did not sanction the procedure. Harbisson stated that 'for me, a cyborg is someone who feels their technology is a part of their biology. They have integrated a device or devices into their body and this has added something to their senses or capability above and beyond what's -currently normal for humans' (Carroll 2014).

Donna Haraway, in her famous essay 'A Cyborg Manifesto' (1984), defines a cyborg as 'a cybernetic organism, a hybrid of machine and organism, a creature of social reality as well as a creature of fiction' (1991: 149). The cyborg's existence, she argues, involves a 'struggle over life and death, but the boundary between science fiction and social reality is an optical illusion'. In fact, she says, 'we are cyborgs. The cyborg is our ontology', and that we are being 'hybrids of machine and organism', and a 'condensed image of both imagination and material reality' (150). For Haraway, cyborgs can no longer be confined to science fiction, and she stresses the importance of the imagination within reality. Aleksandra Przegalinska, however, voices her concerns over such a development:

> I think the goal of transhumanism is to transcend humanity as we know it and move to another level where we would be totally integrated with machines. What is very problematic for many people is that this transcendence through technology is going to lead us to immortality. (Bricis 2017)

By potentially eliminating death as a central factor in our lives, humanity's sense of a finite existence is removed, its value rendered insufficient as a result, since the limits of life imbue it with inherent value.

But as problematic as immortality may prove in this instance, it is not entirely unheard of in the biological world. The strong link society makes between death and biology is quite easily undermined when we turn our attention to the animal kingdom. While American lobster are able to regenerate, growing limbs if they accidentally lose one, the existence of the immortal jellyfish challenges many of our preconceived notions about organic beings that defy death or deterioration. Living organisms such as the immortal jellyfish can grow into a sexually mature adult, and then revert to an immature polyp. Such an organism is classified as a 'biologically immortal' being.

The particular mechanisms surrounding the reasons behind the immortal jellyfish's ultra-longevity are mysterious, and what is more the jellyfish's alien existence is testament to how different humans are from other living organisms, not only in appearance, but in lifespan.

In 2006, Ming the mollusc was found in Iceland when it was dredged up from the water, and subsequently killed. The mollusc was purported to be 507 years old, yet it was also postulated that had it not been brought to the surface, it may have been immortal, that is, not susceptible to death through mere ageing.

The fact that not all living organisms are vulnerable to mortality suggests that mortality itself is not inherently biological in nature. This also suggests that immortality does not necessarily invalidate a machine's claim to potentially be considered an organic life-form. If immortality exists in the biological realm, then it may be acceptable to view immortality as an potential part of a living organism, unsettling the notion that humanity is validated through death. Thus the long held assumption that a biological entity must be subject to mortality is therefore somewhat erroneous, potentially undermining the role that death plays in the existence of humanity.

NON-BIOLOGICAL DEATH

In light of these developments in technology and science, definitions regarding not only the human, but also death, are in the process of being altered irrevocably. Propelled by advancements in AI and cyborg technology, as well as the simple fear of death, the mortal limitations of humanity that previously defined our species are being overcome, meaning that notions of humanity and existence may no longer be as stable as they once were.

The desire for immortality and the development of more human cyborgs has obvious implications for humans. But the act of removing biology from the equation of death also has significant implications for the future of artificial intelligence as well, since the manner in which a robot experiences death does not technically involve any biological process. What this suggests is that as humanity increasingly attempts to defy mortality, not only will the definition of humanity itself become altered, but the notion of death may too change to accommodate a non-biological condition of cessation of being. Robots may in fact be able to be considered dead in a non-biological sense, just as humans who become cyborgs undergo a death that transcends biology. Just as Kurzweil posits that 'non-biological thinking' will exist, so too will the notion of non-biological death become more resonant.

In order to understand what a non-biological death may look like, we first need to understand the fundamentals of what constitutes 'death'. Death is more often understood as the mere cessation of life, so the definition of life, therefore, becomes absolutely paramount to a discussion of what can be considered clinically, philosophically, biologically and legally dead. To claim that a machine has died is not the same as claiming that a human being has died. A computer that no longer works may be considered 'dead', yet its claim to life in the first place would seem to invalidate its claim to death. However, such views ultimately subscribe to preconceived views about what it means to die in the first place.

Unsurprisingly, not much is written on the 'non-human death', or a 'non-biological death'. The ethics surrounding death are still very much tied to humanity, to biology. This is simply because death has always been understood as a strictly biological phenomenon befalling organic matter or beings, since it has been seen to occur to and within living organisms only. Yet although this argument has been historically sustained, it is itself undergoing a process of change as scientists increasingly discuss the potential for a machine to be considered 'alive'.

Erica Borgstrom has argued that while 'death is considered a universal' (2017: 5), it is also something that can vary in regards to conclusive definitions, and she includes 'social death' as a particular approach to understanding mortality. Looking at illnesses such as dementia, Borgstrom argues that 'a unifying feature is that [social death] is used to comment on the way people may be regarded as if they are something other than human or no longer a person' (5).

Discussing social death, Floris Tomasini argues that 'while social death is dependent on having existed, it is not necessarily co-terminus with existing as a biological entity' (2017: 14). This is a significant observation for the purposes of understanding how a machine—evidently a non-biological entity by conventional standards—can still be regarded as undergoing or experiencing a kind of death not yet identified. In fact, Tomasini discusses 'techno-death', 'where machines, like ventilators, take over from biological sub-systems that has permanently and irreversibly failed' (10).

Tomasini also notes that 'less subtly, brain injury, as argued earlier, can lead to narrative inversions in our clinical status: from a living person that is self-conscious and aware of others, to a living human organism which in Persistent Vegetative State (PVS) is not conscious in this way' (14).

The death of a brain is, in the medical field, almost always linked to the death of a human (known controversially as 'brain death'). And the death of a human is almost always seen to occur when their brain—more than any other organ—ceases to function. Since consciousness is considered something that arises within the brain, as I will discuss in the following chapter, an absence or failure of consciousness (rather than, say, an absence of a heart or other bodily organs besides the brain) is linked with an absence of life.

Daniel Wikler, a staff ethicist for the World Health Organization, has argued that it is more logical that death occurs 'when the cerebrum—the centre for consciousness, thoughts and feelings, the properties essential to having a personal identity—[is] destroyed' (Aviv 2018). Rachel Aviv notes that Wikler's argument 'would have rendered a much broader population of patients, including those who could breathe on their own, dead'. But in many cases, including the now-famous case of Jahi McMath—a girl left brain dead in 2013 following complications from a tonsillectomy, but who still shows signs of life and movement—the application of the term and condition 'death' has been met with much ethical discussion.

A lack of consciousness, in McMath's case, does not signify death for her family (while the medical community at large in this case almost uniformly considered the young girl irrevocably dead, the case of which is ongoing). But the link between the brain and life—which dominates medical and legal parlance—is gradually being challenged by those for whom consciousness is not the defining factor signifying life (and its absence signifying death).

D. Alan Shewmon, who was the chief of the neurology department at the Olive View-U.C.L.A. Medical Centre, noted that 'few doctors could confidently articulate why the destruction of one organ was synonymous with death' (Aviv 2018). As Rachel Aviv writes, usually these doctors would argue that these patients 'were still living biological organisms but had lost the capacities that made them human'. This statement is particular insightful, since it makes a crucial distinction between humanity and biology, a distinction that is not usually maintained. The essential link between humanity and biology is questioned, and a human being, in this estimation, can be biologically alive, but has seemingly lost their 'essence' of humanity. By the same token, a machine, being an entity bereft of biological essence, can nevertheless be considered—in theory—a living entity if it comes to reflect values which we ascribe to humans, despite lacking biological origin.

In the cases in which a human being is in a vegetative state, they are biological beings but without consciousness, which often results in a ruling that they are technically 'dead'. The same is often said about robots who lack the capacity for consciousness—an awareness of themselves and the world around them. Yet just as McMath's family believe that Jahi is still alive, since she is breathing and has a heartbeat despite the compromising state of her brain function, so too can we accommodate the notion that a lack of consciousness does not therefore denote the absence of life in a machine.

The President's council on bioethics reconsidered the definition of death in 2008. While it accommodated Shewmon's findings and abandoned the notion that a 'functioning brain was necessary for the body to operate as an "integrated whole"', it maintained that brain destruction still equated death, because such a case meant that a human could no longer 'engage in commerce with the surrounding world', which is 'what an organism does and what distinguishes every organism from non-living things' (Aviv).

Yet not all living beings engage with their surrounding world in the same way. For many mentally impaired people, the aforementioned statement from the council would designate them as legally 'dead'. And as previously noted, we cannot really know the extent of a machine's sense of experience.

For Shewmon, in this case, brain disability does not equate death, saying that McMath is 'an extremely disabled but very much alive teenage girl' (Aviv 2018). In this instance, her disability, for Shewmon, does not negate her claim to life.

The ambiguity that remains around what constitutes death, in these cases, is epitomised in Edmund Pellegrino's statement that the boundaries of death are often determined by a problematic, 'circular reasoning—defining death in terms of life and life in terms of death without a true 'definition' of one or the other' (Aviv).

While life is designated to something that can die, death is ascribed to something that lives. But as consciousness is becoming less and less important for living organisms such as human beings, the existential status of robots in the future may themselves be subject to change, in which case life may not be a necessity in the process of death, rendering death something potentially non-biological in future scenarios. While biological death will, of course, continue to define life and humanity, it may become varied in scope, accommodating newer and different formulations and experiences of death. Just as Jahi McMath can be considered alive without consciousness, so too can the machine that allows her to live be eventually considered something capable of death.

REFERENCES

Aviv, Rachel. 'What Does It Mean to Die?' *The New Yorker*. February 5, 2018. Retrieved February 8, 2018, from https://www.newyorker.com/magazine/2018/02/05/what-does-it-mean-to-die.

Becker, Ernest. *The Denial of Death*. New York: The Free Press, 1973.

Borgstrom, Erica. 'Social Death'. *QJM: An International Journal of Medicine*. Vol. 110, 2017, pp. 5–7.

Bricis, Larissa. 'A Philosopher Predicts How and When Robots Will Destroy Humanity'. *Techly*. September 25, 2017. Retrieved October 11, 2017, from https://www.techly.com.au/2017/09/22/philosopher-predicts-robots-will-destroy-humanity/.

Carroll, Michael. 'Part Human, Part Machine, Cyborgs Are Becoming a Reality'. *Newsweek*. July 31, 2014. Retrieved September 25, 2017, from http://www.newsweek.com/2014/08/08/cyborgs-are-walking-among-us-262132.html.

Colebrook, Claire. *Death of the Post Human: Essays on Extinction, Volume 1*. Ann Arbor: Open Humanities Press, 2014.

Cooter, Roger. 'The Dead Body'. *Companion to Medicine in the Twentieth Century*. Cooter, Roger and Pickstone, John (eds.). London and New York: Routledge, 2003, pp. 469–486.

Cozzolino, Philip J., and Blackie, Laura E. 'I Die, Therefore I Am: The Pursuit of Meaning in the Light of Death'. *The Experience of Meaning in Life: Classical Perspectives, Emerging Themes, and Controversies*. Hicks, Joshua A. (ed.). Netherlands: Springer, 2013, pp. 31–45.

Deleuze, Gilles, and Guattari, Félix. *Anti-oedipus: Capitalism and Schizophrenia*. London and New York: Continuum, 2004.

Fedorov, Nikolai. *What Was Man Created For?: The Philosophy of the Common Task*. London: Honeyglen, 2008.

Fischer, John Martin. *The Metaphysics of Death*. Stanford: Stanford University Press, 1993.

Freud, Sigmund. *The Standard Edition of the Complete Psychological Works of Sigmund Freud: Volume XIV (1914–1916) On the History of the Psycho-analytic Movement, Papers on Metapsychology and Other Works*. London: Vintage, 2001.

Goldman, David. *How Civilizations Die: (And Why Islam Is Dying Too)*. Washington: Regnery, 2011.

Griffin, Andrew. 'Humans Will Become Hybrids by 2030, Says Leading Google Engineer, with Tiny Robots Scurrying Around Our Brain to Help Us Think'. *The Independent*. June 4, 2015. Retrieved September 15, 2017, from http://www.independent.co.uk/life-style/gadgets-and-tech/news/humans-will-become-hybrids-by-2030-says-leading-google-engineer-with-tiny-robots-scurrying-around-10296200.html.

Haraway, Donna. 'A Cyborg Manifesto: Science, Technology, and Socialist Feminism in the Late Twentieth Century'. *Simians, Cyborgs and Women: The Reinvention of Nature*. New York: Routledge, 1991, pp. 149–181.

Heidegger, Martin. *On the Way to Language*. New York: Harper and Row Publishers, 1982.

Heidegger, Martin. *Being and Time*. Albany: New York Press, 2010.

Howarth, Glennys, and Leaman, Oliver. *Encyclopaedia of Death and Dying*. London and New York: Routledge, 2001.

Jacobs, Joseph. 'The Dying of Death'. *Fortnightly Review*. New Series 72, 1899, pp. 264–269.

Kolbert, Elizabeth. *The Sixth Extinction: An Unnatural History*. New York: Henry Holt and Company, 2014.

Lukashevich, Stephen. *N. F. Fedorov (1828–1903): A Study in Russian Eupsychian and Utopian Thought*. Newark: University of Delaware Press, Associated University Presses, 1977.

Prioreschi, Plinio. *A History of Human Responses to Death: Mythologies, Rituals, and Ethics*. Studies in Health and Human Services. Volume 17. Lewiston: The Edwin Mellen Press, 1990.

Tomasini, Floris. *Remembering and Disremembering the Dead: Posthumous Punishment, Harm and Redemption Over Time*. New York: Palgrave Macmillan, 2017.

Treder, Mike. 'Emancipation from Death'. *The Scientific Conquest of Death: Essays on Infinite Lifespans*. The Immortality Institute, 2004, pp. 187–196.

Tucker, Ian. 'Genevieve Bell: "Humanity's Greatest Fear Is About Being Irrelevant"'. *The Guardian*. November 27, 2016. Retrieved September 24, 2017, from https://www.theguardian.com/technology/2016/nov/27/genevieve-bell-ai-robotics-anthropologist-robots.

Warren, Hannah. 'Should We Be Fighting Robots—Or Becoming Them?' *Techly*. August 23, 2016. Retrieved November 12, 2017, from https://www.techly.com.au/2016/08/23/fighting-robots-becoming/.

CHAPTER 3

Machine Consciousness: Ethics and Implications

Abstract This chapter investigates the notion of 'machine consciousness' and the concept of a 'robot life'. The chapter focuses on current debates surrounding the 'hard problem of consciousness', and the potential link between machines and consciousness in science and technology. This chapter also deals with the significant ethical implications of the development of machine life, including the development of autonomous weaponry or 'killer robots', as well as the potential loss of an 'essential' humanity. Finally, this chapter examines the persistence of the 'Frankenstein Complex', before challenging commonplace assumptions about the malevolent potential of a robot species.

Keywords Machine consciousness · Brain · Ethics · Essentialism
Killer robots

CREATING CONSCIOUSNESS

Before asking whether or not a robot or other machine could ever be capable of dying, it is necessary to first discuss the ambiguous nature of a robot or machine consciousness. Since robots are not believed to be able to possess the self-awareness required to understand or undergo 'death', then it would logically follow that a robot is incapable of being considered dead in the human-sense of the term.

© The Author(s) 2018
S. Lyons, *Death and the Machine*,
https://doi.org/10.1007/978-981-13-0335-7_3

Although we do in fact use the word 'dead' to refer to inanimate objects (dead computers, dead car batteries, etc.), we are not evoking the same ethical or semantic significance as the biological notion that 'death' itself carries. But certain developments in both technology and metaphysics allow for a reimagining of the manner in which a particular being is capable of possessing either element of life or death.

So what would a robot life look like? Certainly, it would be difficult to argue that a robot could ever attain a biological, human kind of life. But this claim in and of itself does not remove or undermine the possibility that a robot could, in a certain respect, live. If we reorder the notions of (a) what it means to be human and (b) what actually constitutes life outside the boundaries of humanity or more broadly the organic world, then we may be permitted to welcome the notion of robot life—similar to but distinct from human life. For at the moment we have one primary understanding of what it means to have life, and one primary understanding of what it means to be human, that is, through biology. Yet this book seeks to challenge both assumptions in order to, at the very least, interrogate possible futures of existence for which we do not yet have a name or concept, or what Gilles Deleuze calls the 'people-to-come'. As Deleuze has argued, 'the creation of concepts in itself calls for a future form, for a new earth and people that do not yet exist' (1994: 108). In this way, discussing the extent to which a robot could possess 'life' is imperative to not only understanding the existence of humanity, but in understanding possible futures for the human species.

Methods towards creating robot life remain centred predominantly around the physical. In 2017, researchers from the University of Houston created artificial skin that could enable robots to experience the sense of touch, thereby providing a fundamental but overlooked element in the experience of humanity. But sense of touch, indeed, all of the human senses, do not equate consciousness, and do not solely inform humanity.

Evidently, the notion of 'engineering' life or being able to create consciousness certainly seems paradoxical, completely negating and undermining the essence of consciousness, insofar that consciousness is seen to be something that is born within the human mind and therefore cannot be *artificially* created. The ambiguous nature of consciousness has eluded and confounded philosophers and scientists alike; while it does not have a single conclusive definition, various critics and thinkers have attempted to narrow it down. According to Searle, consciousness is defined as 'inner qualitative, subjective states, and processes of sentience or awareness' (2000: 559). Shared amongst most definitions of consciousness is this state of self-awareness. This self-awareness is almost always said to emerge within the complex structure of the brain, being considered inherently biological; as Christof Koch and Giulio Tononi argue, consciousness is 'part of the natural world' (2008). Hugo Lagercrantz and Jean-Pierre Changeux share this assessment, noting that 'consciousness emerges from special neuronal features in the brain or "neuronal correlates"' (2009: 255). This is a crucial distinction, since there is an assumed (and somewhat unsurprising) link between biology and consciousness, in which consciousness cannot exist without a human or, at least, a biological brain.

Yet Koch and Tononi argue that it is evidently difficult to describe just exactly what consciousness entails, however: 'Pressed for a pithy definition, we might call [consciousness] the ineffable and enigmatic inner life of the mind' (2008). But they maintain that consciousness is interconnected with the mechanisms of a human brain: 'We know it arises in the brain, but we don't know how or where in the brain. We don't even know if it requires specialized brain cells (or neurons) or some sort of special circuit arrangement of them' (2008).

Hence, consciousness is generally perceived in the same vein as humanity: belonging to a biological realm; a machine is thought to be unable to possess consciousness because consciousness depends on a biological brain to exist.

But consciousness pertains to more than mere thought; for many theorists, the emphasis needs to be placed on feeling and emotion, rather than simply intellect. Computers have intellect, can predict, and can beat humans at chess. But intellectual capability is not in and of itself purely human, and the fact that a machine can beat a human at chess does not confer upon it consciousness. So the term artificial intelligence is less significant in discussions of consciousness, since it is not intelligence alone that informs humanity. This is where the debate regarding an animal's intellectual capability also becomes useful. By that same token, a lack of consciousness does not invalidate humanity; a person in a coma—whose mental faculties, as with the case of Jahi McMath, appear to be unresponsive—may not be conscious, and yet this does not usually impact their status as a human. It may, as I discussed in the previous chapter, be shown to invalidate their status as a living being, and we describe this state as 'vegetative', and yet they are, more or less, understood as being intrinsically human despite the loss of a functioning cerebral cortex.

The Global Neuronal Workspace distinguishes five processes involved in consciousness, including evaluative systems (value), attentional systems (focusing), motor systems (future), perceptual systems (present), and long-term memory (past). Crucially, humans do not appear to be *born* with self-awareness. According to Lagercrantz and Changeux, 'a simple definition of consciousness is sensory awareness of the body, the self, and the world' (2009: 255). Discussing a foetus, they note that it may be aware of its body: 'It reacts to touch, smell, and sound, and shows facial expressions responding to external stimuli. However, these reactions are probably preprogrammed and have a subcortical non-conscious origin' (255). This leads us to the question of how and when self-awareness actually develops, a question that Koch has asked: 'when does the magical journey of consciousness begin?' (Koch 2009). He notes that while newborns lack self-awareness, a baby 'processes complex visual stimuli and attends to sounds and sights in its world', meaning that a baby has 'some basic level of unreflective, present-oriented consciousness'. He posits, also, that 'many of the circuit elements necessary for consciousness are in place by the third trimester' (2009).

As seen in the lively debates surrounding abortion, the presence of 'life', however ambiguous, is seen to be the determining factor behind questions of the foetus' claim to be human and therefore, its claim to be born. If we take consciousness to be synonymous with a claim to life, then a foetus may not necessarily be considered fundamentally human. Even newborns lack the necessary level of consciousness to be considered fully human. 'Newborn infants', Lagercrantz and Changeux note, 'display features characteristic of what may be referred to as basic consciousness and they still have to undergo considerable maturation to reach that level of adult consciousness' (2009: 255).

This is where the human and the machine may start to appear fundamentally different in the gaining of consciousness; although not yet possessing adult consciousness, most newborn babies will invariably attain consciousness as they mature. A machine, on the other hand, is seen to lack this crucial sense of growth and maturity that would see consciousness develop (or, we at least assume as much). Even so-called 'immortal jellyfish', as discussed in the previous chapter, are first required to reach adulthood before they can revert to an earlier form.

Although it may seem doubtful that a robot could ever develop in the way that a human being does, recent developments in the field of robotics show that biological phenomena such as natural selection may also apply to machinery. As Brodbeck et al. note, natural selection may eventually occur in robotics in the form of 'artificial evolution'; 'today's machines', they write, are 'highly restricted to their initial morphological configurations' (2015: 1), but that 'it is still a question whether machines can achieve a similar level of adaptability by adjusting their morphologies' in the way that animals previously have. This is enabled by constructing a 'mother' robot that can design and build its own 'children' and improve the performance of future generations without human intervention: 'Machines are physically constructed and their performance is analysed without simulation and human intervention to incrementally improve their functionality' (2015: 2).

It seems possible, then, for a robot to undergo a process of development, adaptation or evolution beyond its initial construction. This has led to the development of robot adaptation, or 'evolutionary robotics', which 'allows for the creation of autonomous robots without human intervention' (University of Cambridge 2015). Brodbeck et al.'s research shows that 'as in nature, evolution in robots takes place through 'mutation', where components of one gene are modified or single genes are added or deleted, and 'crossover', where a new genome is formed by merging genes from two individuals' (University of Cambridge 2015).

However, robot adaptation does not take place in the same way as it does for a human: 'Machines are not adaptable in the same way. They are essentially stuck in one shape for their entire 'lives', and it's uncertain whether changing their shape would make them more adaptable to changing environments' (University of Cambridge 2015).

Yet this still does not help in wholly separating the human from the machine, since there are many humans who do sufficiently mature and who do not reach the same level of adult consciousness, potentially meaning that *it is not consciousness alone* that determines or validates humanity. Fallibility, unpredictability, fragility and ignorance, in fact, all those things which appear diametrically opposed to the notion of intelligence, are elements that can be used to define or categorise humanity. Humans are intelligent in regards to self-awareness, and yet they are more often marked by their flaws than their abilities, which accords with Masahiro Mori's notions of the uncanny valley, which I will discuss later in this chapter.

Philosophers such as Karl Marx and Friedrich Nietzsche argued against seeing consciousness as the centre of the economy of life. For others, such as Daniel Dennett, consciousness isn't necessarily inherently tied to the physical. Famously, Dennett argues that consciousness is an 'illusion', an argument that was not widely embraced in either the humanities or neurosciences. David Chalmers and Thomas Nagel, in particular, were critical of Dennett's work *Consciousness Explained* (1993), in which he argues for the case of robot with consciousness.

Chalmers, on the other hand, has discussed the 'hard problem of consciousness', that is, the esoteric link between the physical brain and our experiences, arguing that consciousness may be existent in the universe at large, what is known as *panpsychism*. Panpsychism refers to subjective experience that is ubiquitous and possibly found in all things. This means that humans and inanimate objects both experience some form of consciousness, but to different degrees, again highlighting the notion that consciousness is related to but distinct from thought alone.

Indeed, if we subscribe to a panpsychic approach, in which consciousness is potentially existent in the universe more broadly, then the argument could be made that robots may eventually develop consciousness.

This in itself is a kind of evolution, by which the structure of humanity adapts to technological change or evolution. Future humans will indeed be hybrid. But this frightens us less than the prospect of actually developing an entirely new species, through embracing a promethean role in society that follows a pattern of destruction and creation.

Yet in his book *Mankind in Transition* (1993), Masse Bloomfield argues that 'it is impossible for modern man to differentiate into a new species on earth' (16). Niles Eldredge and Ian Tattersall similarly argued, in 1982, that 'there is precious little chance of anything major happening in our physical evolution' (1982: 185).

Such views, however, seem outdated in the contemporary landscape and in light of these developments in robotic technology. Certainly, the advent of cyborgs has challenged the extent to which humans will remain purely biological in nature.

In light of the hard problem of consciousness, theorists continue to debate the extent to which a machine might ever be able to attain some identifiable semblance of consciousness. While there are those who dismiss speculation on the topic owing to the assumption that robots will never gain the familiar kinds of consciousness to which we are already familiar, others, such as Christof Koch, chief scientific officer of the Allen Institute for Brain Science in Seattle, claim that robots could indeed become self-aware: 'If you were to build a computer that has the same circuitry as the brain, this computer would also have consciousness associated with it. It would feel like something to be this computer' (Regalado 2014). He notes, however, that 'the same is not true for digital simulations'. For Koch, simulation will not equate reality, because a computer simulation of consciousness does not feel what it is to *be*.

The problem of simulation was famously addressed by John Searle in his Chinese Room thought experiment in 1980. The experiment features a computer inside a room that is given Chinese characters as input and also produces Chinese characters convincingly enough to pass what is known as the Turing test—a test that determines the ability of a machine to exhibit intelligent behaviour indistinguishable from a human. Searle asks us to imagine ourselves as a Chinese speaker, one who is speaking to the computer from outside the room, without the knowledge that they are speaking to a computer, convinced that the computer is, in fact, human.

Searle asks whether the machine can actually understand Chinese, or whether it is merely simulating Chinese without understanding it— what's known as strong and weak AI respectively. Searle's point is that simulation does not equate reality, and that the simulation of thought is irrevocably different to actual thought, no matter how sophisticated the programming.

Searle's approach has influenced the popular notion that one can 'program' intelligent thought, but that intelligent thought does not equate consciousness. Where, then, might consciousness be located? For Koch, consciousness is not necessarily located in the primary visual cortex; for Koch, consciousness can be found in the *prefrontal* cortex, where short-term memory and attention are produced, which contribute to what is called 'visual consciousness'.

If, as Lagercrantz argues, consciousness is dependent on 'neuronal features', we must then ask whether these can truly be artificially created, despite consciousness seeming to emerge naturally. In his book *Future Smart*, James Canton posits that the combination of artificial intelligence and the human brain could create what he calls 'synthetic minds', possessing two critical but distinct elements of natural and artificial origin. Using neuroscience in conjunction with technology, Canton proposes that 'neurological models will lead to designing new neuromimetic cognitive devices that could be used to create minds for virtual cyberspace entities and mobile autonomous robotics' (2015: 344). He notes that the 'long path to creating artificial intelligence may finally be realised by the convergence of neuroscience, neurotechnology, and cybernetics'

(345). Canton predicts that this sort of artificial intelligence will be a reality by the year 2020. But such developments, he concedes, will produce a number of legal and ethical concerns:

> The long-range scenarios predicated by this forecast assume an ethical and social responsibility for which we have yet to establish rules. We have much work to do as scientists, lawyers, health care providers, and policy makers to prepare for the imminent neurofuture. (345)

While theorists like Koch aspire to find empirical evidence of consciousness, others see it as something that cannot be explained away by science. In his compelling article 'Consciousness without Bodies', Bjorn Beijnon discusses the respective approaches to consciousness between the neuroscience and philosophy industries. The dependence that neuroscience has on visual 'facts', he argues, confines the industry to an empirical 'truth':

> In the last couple of years, neuroscience made us believe that a study of the human brain would give a direct correlation with studies on consciousness. "Being conscious" or "making a conscious decision" could be measured through visual tools. These images are, however, stripped of any imagination; these images represent a pinch of the truth and are therefore served as facts.

He also notes that neuroscience 'no longer has a monopoly on the truth in brain imagery, but it has to conform itself to the truth that comes out of the research its findings'. In contrast, Beijnon argues that certain philosophies such as Brain Studies 'keep on questioning the correlation between human consciousness and the brain'. More and more it seems as though philosophers, more so than scientists, are in a position to discuss the nature of consciousness since, as Beijnon puts it, imagination strengthens insight.

As Agustín Fuentes and Aku Visala note, 'even if the scientific quest for human nature ends up being futile, who is to say that there cannot be an account of human nature that is not scientific?' (2016: 30). They note that 'many a philosopher (and theologian) might say that there is an essential human nature but it is not accessible in any direct way by science'.

For Dennett, machine consciousness is a very real possibility, but one that is not particularly attractive to others: 'other people, however, find the implication that there could be, in principle, a conscious robot so incredible that it amounts in their eyes to the *reductio ad absurdum* of my theory'

(1993: 432). Dennett offers a useful observation on the distinction between speculation and reality: 'it's obvious that no teddy bear is conscious, but it's not really obvious that no robot could be. What is obvious is just that it's hard to imagine how they could be'. Since, he writes, people find it difficult to imagine how a robot could be conscious, they are reluctant to imagine such a creation. But, he argues, 'it's just as difficult to imagine how a human brain could support consciousness' (433).

Chalmers, too, has expressed an openness to the idea of a conscious robot: 'Could a robot be conscious in the way that a human being is, or do you need a special biology to be conscious? I was always on the side of the robots. That's not to say there's no mystery about consciousness' (Keane 2017).

While the link between technology and mortality is usually discussed by providing immortality for humans by uploading their consciousness to a technological device, the notion of 'robot life' may also take the form of constructing biological matter (if at all possible) and inserting it into a robot. Yet regardless of the technology needed to make such a development a reality, in any case we become confronted with several hypothetical situations that challenge, undermine, or destabilise conventional notions of what it means to be human.

For Amitav Ghosh, 'we are confronted suddenly with a new task: that of finding other ways in which to imagine the unthinkable beings and events of this era' (2016: 33). Ghosh argues that it is particularly necessary to conceive of new beings in the era of climate change, saying: 'to imagine other forms human existence is exactly the challenge that is posed by the climate crisis' (128).

ETHICS AND ESSENTIALISM

What are some of the ethical implications that 'robot life' and 'robot death' evoke? Why would we *choose* to ascribe life to a machine, especially in an era where the fragility of humanity is at the forefront of much philosophical and scientific discourse? In light of the aforementioned discussion, in which machine consciousness appears theoretically possible, we are then confronted with an unusual and, distinctly uncomfortable dilemma. For if life becomes something that is biochemically or technologically engineered, then we begin to lose the foundational basis upon which an 'essential humanity' is based. Indeed, the ascribing of life and death onto a machine is fraught with conceptual and ethical difficulties that potentially challenge and undermine previous distinctions that have favoured either biological humanity or the notion that life and death itself are purely biological. In fact, much of the resistance to such a theory stems in part, I believe, from these humanist desires.

If we permit robots the 'gift of death', or sanction any notion of a 'robot life', for some people we may subsequently risk devaluing human life. This is already the case in certain circumstances, such as the euthanasia debate between humans and animals. But in such a circumstance, the 'sanctity of life' rhetoric defines and dictates such resolute objections to human euthanasia, with 'life', in this instance, referring predominantly to the sanctity of *human* life, above other entities.

As Dennett himself has noted, there are several reasons people have for 'believing in the impossibility of conscious robots' that relate to this notion of essentialism. He writes that for some people, 'robots are artefacts, and consciousness abhors an artefact; only something natural, born not manufactured, could exhibit genuine consciousness' (156). In response to this assumption, Dennett argues that 'it is tempting to dismiss this claim with derision, and in some of its forms, derision is just what it deserves'. Dennett notes that the notion of 'origin essentialism' can be seen as what he calls 'origin chauvinism', arguing against the notion that one's origin uniformly determines their ability to be a conscious being.

Romantic, humanist attitudes about an essential human nature, or what Wilhem von Humboldt considered 'human essence' and the ideal of humanity, have dictated approaches to living organisms and the superiority of the human being in the fabric of life. Yet Enlightened philosophers such as Denis Diderot, Søren Kierkegaard, Immanuel Kant, David Hume and Adam Smith rejected this conception of an 'essential' human nature. Indeed, as Vyverberg points out, both Diderot and Jean-Jacques Rousseau agreed that 'this essential, benevolent human nature later had become overlaid with mischievous artificiality and affectation' (1989: 47). Indeed, the notion of an essential human nature now appears naïve in its view, since it neglects other aspects of human behaviour that fall short of what 'moral' philosophers like Aristotle described as 'human excellence' (discussed in Chapter 4). If we nevertheless abide by an essentialist or humanist view, we must also concede that humans have much to answer for in regards to behaviour. Or, as Christopher Berry noted: 'To believe that there is an essential human nature is to believe that there is one possible description of Man that renders all possible descriptions commensurable' (1986: 127).

Hannah Arendt, too, at the beginning of her work *The Human Condition* (1998), argues against an essential human nature, positing: 'nothing entitles us to assume that man has a nature or essence in the same sense as other things' (1998: 10), while also claiming that human nature 'does not exist' (193).

With these views in mind, it becomes problematic to instantly invalidate a robot's claim to have some kind of 'essence', since philosophers have long challenged humanity's claim to its own perceived 'essence', an essence almost always exclusively linked to the biological. If, then, a claim could still be made that there exists any kind of 'essence', it may no longer have ties to human biology alone, but could be extended to that of the artificial, what Masahiro Mori calls the 'buddha-nature' of robots (also discussed at length in Chapter 4).

More recently, the notion that there is an underlying *human* essence has continued to be challenged. In his discussion on the relationship between humans and non-humans, Timothy Morton argues that 'humans have indeed been alienated from something, but not from some stable, bland underlying essence' (2017: 17). Indeed, as Sherry Turkle writes, 'we find ourselves in a complex position in our attitudes towards biological life. There is a preoccupation with genetics as a predicator of success and failure in life, thus emphasising the importance of biological ties' (1995: 170). 'Genetic essentialism', she argues, requires us to 'emphasise DNA as the carrier of our biological connections'. She notes, however, that 'biological essentialism puts computational objects on the other side of a line, even as ideas from emergent AI and A-Life challenge the line itself'.

Tellingly, such attitudes towards the existential nature of robots is changing somewhat. As I previously discussed in the introduction, robots are increasingly being discussed in quite essentialist terms in the media. One of the most prominent examples of this involves the remote-controlled robots who were sent into the Fukushima Daiichi Nuclear Power Plant in Japan, the site of the 2011 meltdown. In 2016, several reports were published stating that the robots had in fact 'died' from radioactive poisoning. The robots begun to rust from the radiation, and subsequently shut down. But the actual reporting on the event was significant insofar as it framed the state of the robots as one of 'death'. They did not simply shut down, fail, or stop working. They had 'died'. Actual robot deaths are rarely, if ever, reported in the media, simply because, as previously noted, robots are not accommodated in the terminology of 'death'. Yet this development is quite modest in scope, and does not confer upon robots a sense of consciousness or morality.

It does, however, suggest that as AI technology develops, so too do our attitudes regarding what actually constitutes life, and the rhetoric surrounding death.

KILLER ROBOTS

Although there is uncertainty around labelling a machine 'alive' or 'dead', there are numerous instances where machines are readily linked to other severe ethical dilemmas. More and more robots have been blamed, in the media, for causing the death of humans, and this has provoked numerous ethical discussions regarding the responsibility of a machine.

The first known person to have been killed by a robot was Robert Williams, in 1979. Williams died after being struck in the head by an industrial robot arm at the Ford Motor Company factory, in Flat Rock, Michigan. His family subsequently sued Litton Industries, the manufacturers of the industrial robot, and in 1983 they were awarded $10 million dollars. The court had ruled that proper safety measures had not been taken to prevent the accident. Two years later, Japanese engineer Kenji Urada was killed after a broken robot pushed him into a grinding machine at a Kawasaki Heavy Industries plant in Japan.

The most recent death as a result of robot interference occurred in July 2015, again in Michigan. Maintenance technician Wanda Holbrook had her skull crushed after robotic machinery at the Ventra Ionia Main plant moved into her section of the plant and 'loaded a trailer attachment assembly part onto her head'. Cells in the section are usually separated by safety doors, though a malfunction enabled the robot to enter Holbrook's section, trapping her against the assembly part, killing her instantly.

In March 2017, Holbrook's husband, William Holbrook, filed a wrongful death complaint[1] in the Michigan Federal Court against five American robotics companies, including Prodomax, Flex-N-Gate, FANUC, Nachi and Lincoln Electric.

---

[1] See 'Factory worker killed by rogue robot, says widowed husband in lawsuit', *News. com* (17 March 2017), http://www.news.com.au/technology/factory-worker-killed-by-rogue-robot-says-widowed-husband-in-lawsuit/news-story/13242f7372f9c4614bc-c2b90162bd749 (accessed 26 July 2017).

In both Williams' and Holbrook's cases, blame was ultimately levelled against the flawed, human-designed safety measures that were in place. Evidently, none of the cases involved a robot or piece of machinery that knowingly caused the deaths of the workers. Yet reportage on Holbrook's death in particular framed the death in a menacing manner by claiming that the robot 'went rogue'. Holbrook's husband's claim that the robot should not have been able to enter the section in which his wife was working was subsequently translated as the robot 'going rogue'. *The Independent, News.com, The Telegraph, The Daily Mail, The New York Daily News* and *The Mirror* were just some of the media outlets that specifically reported on the robot going rogue. In contrast, *Detroit Free Press*, a *USA Today* subsidiary, reported that human error was ultimately to blame in the case, and did not phrase the accident as a robot going rogue.

The disparity in media reporting regarding the robot involved in Holbrook's death tellingly suggests that the fear of robots, and the suspicion with which society often views robotic machinery, dominates media discourse. Deaths as a result of robots is, of course, unusual and is certainly cause for investigation. But none of the robots involved, evidently, possessed self-awareness. The particular use of the word 'rogue' in media reporting in Holbrook's case clearly taps into the sensationalism and the added drama and unusualness of a robot accidentally killing a human, even if the death, of course, was in no way intentional or, in fact, rogue.

The topic of a robot's responsibility in health care and warfare has been of interest to a number of robotic ethics scholars. In a speech he gave at the United Nations Conference of Conventional Weapons, Professor Peter Asaro described death by a robot as something that intrudes upon a human being's dignity, stating: 'As a matter of the preservation of human morality, dignity, justice and law we cannot accept an automated system making the decision to take a human life' (2012: 708). The logic behind such a statement is suggestive of the (unsurprising) discrepancy between robots and humans, ultimately suggesting that being killed by a robot lacks the same philosophical resonance as being killed by a living being. He further argues that dignity is 'a notion that we have about what it means to be human that we all share and that can be threatened, and we can suffer indignities'.

Death by robot, therefore, is understood as undignified because there is no biological being behind the death, and in order for one's death to be dignified, it must be caused by a conscious being. Just as robots are seen as incapable of undergoing or experiencing death, so too is the human death as a result of robotics understood in ways that deviate from standard conventions surrounding death. As Michael C. Horowitz argues,

> While in an esoteric sense, the idea that there is something undignified about dying at the hands of a machine resonates, why is being shot through the head or heart and instantly killed by a machine necessarily worse than being bludgeoned, lit on fire, or killed by a cruise missile strike? The dignity argument has emotional resonance, which is why it is important to take it seriously. (2016: 13)

Asaro is one of the spokespersons for the international Campaign to Stop Killer Robots. He is also co-founder and vice-chair of the International Committee for Robot Arms Control. Robotic warfare is one of the most notable and controversial issues surrounding the development of artificial intelligence.

The concern levelled against robots in this case revolves less around robots undermining an essential humanity, and more about the existential detachment that ensues from potentially being killed by that which has no biological underpinnings. Death is seen to only have meaning in a biological setting, and to die from an autonomous machine results is a deprivation of dignity, as well as the notion of being potentially robbed of a legitimate death. This is a particularly worrying issue in regards to the development of autonomous AI.

THE FRANKENSTEIN COMPLEX: FEAR OF THE ROBOT

Because of these very real and legitimate concerns, broader attitudes regarding artificially-intelligent robots are more cautionary than positive. Such attitudes are often reflected in popular culture. When Isaac Asimov's famous work *I, Robot* was adapted for film in 2004, its most significant deviation from the plot revolved around its portrayal of robots as menacing figures who violently turn on their creators. This representation was in stark contrast to both Asimov's book and the author's own views on the presentation of robots in popular culture. In Asimov's novel, there are no instances of robots becoming violent and/or rebellious. The book contains Asimov's famous Three Laws of Robotics, outlining the capabilities of artificial intelligence that have since defined the robotic industry's contemporary approach to robots. The three laws are as follows:

- A robot may not injure a human being or, through inaction, allow a human being to come to harm
- A robot must obey the orders given it by human beings except where such orders would conflict with the First Law
- A robot must protect its own existence as long as such protection does not conflict with the First or Second Laws

Many researchers have discussed implementing these same rules with the introduction of artificial intelligence in everyday scenarios, showing the extent of Asimov's influence.

In response to the continued representation or robots in a negative manner, Asimov coined the term 'Frankenstein Complex', to describe the fear losing control of our own mechanical, technological creations. The fear of robots is one of the most popular and well-known tropes in both science fiction and, now, in everyday life. Unlike the fear of death, the fear of robots is not necessarily based on the unknown, but on the implications that robots have for previously stable definitions of humanity. The physical similarities between humans and robots, and the robot's ability to mimic human behaviour are symptomatic of a seemingly innate suspicion regarding robots. The increasing life-like appearance of humanoid robots, and the subsequent unnerving responses that they arouse, strongly accords with Masahiro Mori's theory of what he calls the 'uncanny valley'.

Mori originally coined the term *Bukimi no Tani Genshō*, before it was translated and became popularised in Jasia Reichardt's book *Robots: Fact, Fiction and Prediction* (1978). Yet Jeremy Hsu argues that the original phrase is more accurately translated as 'the valley of eeriness'. The term refers to the particular feelings that the sight of inanimate, human-like objects provoke, based on the degree of physical similarity between humans and the object in question (including robots, dolls, etc.). According to Reichardt, the more the object seamlessly resembles a human, 'the more affection or feeling of familiarity it can engender' (1978: 26). Yet she also argues that 'the imitation of human exteriors may lead to unexpected effects and unpleasant surprises'. Discussing prosthetics and artificial limbs, Reichardt argues that people may get an 'uncanny feeling' when looking at a hand that looks real but is revealed to be artificial. Once a person would realise that the hand is artificial, the level of familiarity decreases, corresponding to the graph of the 'uncanny valley', determined by the proximity between familiarity and similarity.

For Reichardt, the placement of an object or being (such as a Bunraku toy or a human-shaped robot) in the 'uncanny valley' graph often depends on motion; robots that exhibit very human-like movements seamlessly register as more familiar than a robot whose movements are very basic. 'Movement where we anticipate stillness and stillness where we expect movement is upsetting', Reichardt notes. 'If anything at all goes wrong, either with an artificial hand or a smiling robot, those witnessing the event shudder, and the particular devices immediately drop into the uncanny valley'.

Such responses to robots that only *partly* resemble humans appear to stem from the basic fear of difference, and again reinforces ideas about 'authentic' humans and 'legitimate' behaviour. The same feelings of unfamiliarity, awkwardness and eeriness can be found when engaging with or encountering humans with varied mental or physical disabilities, and the same flawed standards of 'normality' and normal behaviour resurface, reasserting one predominant manner of being authentically human. Any deviations from supposedly normal behaviour is dismissed, distrusted, ignored or avoided. This includes unpredictability in movement or sound. And yet it is this unpredictability that often characterises humans themselves.

Such concerns present us with another ironic issue in regards to the future of robotics, in which society is encouraged to embrace cyborgs, while being repelled by them at the same time. Figures such as Elon Musk and Stephen Hawking are wary of the improvements in artificial intelligence, and promote augmenting the human through technology in order to avoid becoming obsolete. As discussed in Chapter 2, Elon Musk has stated that humans ought to become cyborgs in order to avoid becoming inferior to vastly more intelligent robots. This is another primary reason for fearing robots—the notion that they will come to dominate humanity. Such a concern is also shared by Stephen Hawking.

In contrast to the fear regarding autonomous weapons, in which the fear is understandably linked to security and safety, this particular anxiety corresponds to the insecurity of being human and, therefore, vulnerable to fragility. This is where seemingly innate dystopian fears come to the fore.

Philosopher Aleksandra Przegalinska has argued that the potential for disaster likely outweighs any 'utopian' possibility. She argues:

The best outcome we can count on is a situation where all these programs become really good at what they're doing but don't gain consciousness – so they serve us, augment processes, optimise our work, take some of the work we have been doing and generate new kinds of jobs for us. We don't become unnecessary, jobless humans sitting here and doing nothing; we do have work, and the work we don't want to do is done by machines. (Bricis 2017)

This emphasis on 'machine labour' also defines many fears regarding artificial intelligence; despite being created to specifically perform labour, the corresponding fear of people losing their jobs (not just their existential validation).

Przegalinska expresses concern over what she calls the more likely scenario, that is, that robots 'gain consciousness and don't want to be instrumentalised and treated as machines'. It is interesting that in such cases, consciousness is almost uniformly aligned with either rambunctiousness or disobedience that is subsequently considered something *negative*. Such assumptions unwittingly imply that the basis of consciousness is a sense of disobedience. In this way, the thing we fear—robots disobeying orders and programming—is that which would enable their sentience. Once robots disobey, they not only signal the beginning of a potential elimination of humanity, but the end of 'our' presumed authority as cultural animals. As Genevieve Bell notes, we fear irrelevance, not just elimination.

One of the most famous humanoid robots currently in existence is SoftBank's Pepper robot, developed in 2014. The robot was developed to interpret human emotions, and has an approximate operation time of 12 hours when used at the shop. Many companies have employed the Pepper robot such as Pizza Hut, Nestle and Mastercard. The robots can take orders, offer information and answer customer enquiries.

Yoseph Bar-Cohen and David Hanson discuss the manufacturing of human-like robots. They note that 'presently, even the most realistic robots may seem somewhat dead, because, in many ways, they are' (2009: 103). This line of thinking presupposes that robots are, even in their active state, already dead by way of not being alive in the biological sense. Bar-Cohen and Hanson distinguish between the human and the robot while also noting the ways in which the robot 'mirrors' human traits:

> [Robots] are only partly aware, and they shut down instead of going to sleep. They can also break. These flaws in their humanlike appearance can remind us of our own mortality. They also suggest the act of impersonating humans, conveying the threat of an imposter. However, if we remove these flaws to make them friendly, attractive, and seemingly alive, then the level of realism may not matter. (103)

This helps to explain the resonance of a phenomenon like the uncanny valley, since it provokes and weakens certain assumptions about what it means to be human. Flaws are understood as fundamentally human, and thus the actions of a robot who misbehaves or malfunctions may allude to our own humanity. And just as a robot reminds us of ourselves, so too do our conventional beliefs about the essential stability of humanity become undermined. The similarities between robots and humans may prove threatening to a species that has long benefited from an enviable and unquestioned position in history. In an era that is being described as the 'Anthropocene', the introduction of robots that mimic and impersonate humans fundamentally destabilises and restructures presumed ideas of existence.

Other theorists predict that robots, rather than rebelling against their creators, will be subject to widespread prejudice. In his paper on the Frankenstein Complex and Asimov's Three Laws of Robotics, Lee McCauley notes that 'public fear will be the biggest hurdle for intelligent robots to overcome' (9). He argues that the hesitance regarding the ability to create life through technology stems from quasi-religious notions 'that there are some things that only God should know', with the giving of life being divine in origin. But life, he says:

> ...is deeper than merely animation; it is the imparting of a soul. For centuries, scientists and laymen alike have looked to distinct abilities of humans as evidence of our uniqueness – of our superiority over other animals. Perhaps instinctively, this search has centred almost exclusively on cognitive capacities. (9)

For McCauley, communication and certain social constructs have contributed to this popular idea of 'what makes humans special'. Consequently, he notes, 'many have used this same argument to delineate humans as the only creatures that possess a soul'. We see this sense of essential and biological privilege at work every day, between human rights and animals rights, between human actions and environmental devastation. And, we are seeing it increasingly between human existence and the development of artificial life, which has only strengthened, in some areas, the 'uniqueness' with which humans view themselves.

In response to such developments, Asimov's laws have proved useful in delineating the presence of robots in lawful society, despite the evident ambiguities therein. Researchers such as James Kuffner point to the difficulty in encoding such moral behaviour into a robot, which usually deals only in 'logical or numerical problems' (cited in McCauley: 10). Yet the ability to contradict these laws, in certain cases, is also an important yet problematic factor. As Aaron Sloman writes, the development of artificial intelligence can be discussed through utilitarian philosophy and the fact that 'what harms one may benefit another, etc., and preventing harm to one individual can cause harm to another' (2006). This therefore extends ordinary logic and the deontological notion of 'duty-based' ethics.

But researchers are discussing ways in which to potentially solve or improve these laws. While Roger Clarke has proposed additional laws to fill in certain gaps (1994), others, such as Bill Joy, have proposed that scientists and engineers 'adopt a strong code of ethical conduct resembling the Hippocratic Oath' when developing these AI (2000). As McCauley writes, 'there is still the possibility of technology misuse and irresponsibility on the part of robotics and AI researchers that, while not likely to result in the obliteration of humanity, could be disastrous for the people directly involved' (2007: 14).

The link people frequently make between the development of consciousness and a state of anarchy offers compelling insight into the workings of humanity's pessimism regarding the precise implications of consciousness. The fear that is aligned to machine consciousness (rather than, say, *human* consciousness) is at once surprising and amusing.

It is interesting, for instance, to hear robot expert Francesca Rossi discuss the ethics surrounding robot behaviour. In August 2017, Rossi appeared on Australian television, discussing the need to teach robots right from wrong, in order to maintain 'ethical AI'. In the same week, Michael Cardomone became the first man in Australia to be sentenced to life in prison without the possibility of parole for the rape and murder of Karen Chetcuti. Chetcuti's sister, Leny Verbunt, declared that Cardomone was 'not even a human being'; such sentiments are not uncommon in such brutal cases, in which family members comment on the perpetrator's actions as falling short of the characteristics of humanity.

While Rossi's comments reflect the broader fears relating to the future of robotics in society, the timing of her announcement alongside Cardomone's sentence—which was completely coincidental—should reframe the manner in which we approach discussions on ethics, right and wrong, and good and evil with regards to robots. It seems too much to hope that a human might aspire to learn the difference between right and wrong, and good and evil, before a robot does. In such cases, we already ought to have a fear of *us*, of humanity and the immoral, inhumane manners in which humans already often function.

Indeed, this is precisely what Sloman has discussed in relation to the implementation of an external value system on robots. 'It is unlikely', he notes, 'that intelligent machines could possibly produce more dreadful behaviour towards humans than humans already produce towards each other' (2006). Even in the most civilised places, he argues, we see humans acting in ways that others have imagined robots will act towards us. In fact, Sloman argues that 'the more intelligent the machines are, the less likely they are to produce all the dreadful behaviours motivated by religious intolerance, nationalism, racialism, greed, and sadistic enjoyment of the suffering of others' (2006).

Yet this also may seem to counter the possibility that a robot could indeed achieve human consciousness, since human consciousness seems, irrevocably and lamentably, tied to many of these characteristics of sadism, greed, and intolerance. In this respect, perhaps a robot may be able to gain, develop or acquire consciousness, but one distinct from that of a human consciousness, once again opening a dialogue on the notion that consciousness is purely and fundamentally human.

Robots indeed do not possess the level of awareness needed for complete sentience, and thus cannot, in this line of thinking, be considered meaningfully alive. Popular culture has framed the robotic journey to sentience as dependent, ironically enough, on a moment of technological fallibility, a glitch as it were. It is the fallibility of both humanity and technology that seems to be able to give birth to the sentient robot, permitting either different ways in which to be human, or different ways in which to die, promoting ideas about non-biological death (technological death), or non-biological humanity.

REFERENCES

Arendt, Hannah. *The Human Condition.* Chicago: University of Chicago Press, 1998.
Asaro, Peter. 'On Banning Autonomous Weapon Systems: Human Rights, Automation, and the Dehumanization of Lethal Decision-Making'. *International Review of the Red Cross.* Vol. 94, No. 886, 2012, pp. 687–709.

Bar-Cohen, Yoseph, and Hanson, David. *The Coming Robot Revolution: Expectations and Fears About Emerging Intelligent, Humanlike Machines.* New York: Springer, 2009.

Berry, Christopher J. *Human Nature.* London: Macmillan, 1986.

Bloomfield, Masse. *Mankind in Transition: A View of the Distant Past, the Present and the Far Future.* Canoga Park: Masefield Books, 1993.

Bricis, Larissa. 'A Philosopher Predicts How and When Robots Will Destroy Humanity'. *Techly.* September 25, 2017. Retrieved October 11, 2017, from https://www.techly.com.au/2017/09/22/philosopher-predicts-robots-will-destroy-humanity/.

Brodbeck, Luzius, Hauser, Simon, and Iida, Fumiya. 'Morphological Evolution of Physical Robots Through Model-Free Phenotype Development'. *PLoS One.* Vol. 10, No. 6, 2015.

Canton, James. *Future Smart: Managing the Game-Changing Trends That Will Transform Your World.* Boston: Da Capo Press, 2015.

Clarke, Roger. '"Asimov's Laws of Robotics: Implications for Information Technology, Part 2." Institute of Electrical and Electronics Engineers'. *Computer.* Vol. 27, No. 1, 1994, pp. 57–65.

Deleuze, Gilles, and Guattari, Félix. *What Is Philosophy?* London: Verso, 1994.

Dennett, Daniel. *Consciousness Explained.* London: Penguin, 1993.

Eldredge, Niles, and Tattersall, Ian. *The Myths of Human Evolution.* New York: Columbia University Press, 1982.

Fuentes, Agustín, and Visala, Aku. *Conversations on Human Nature.* London and New York: Routledge, 2016.

Ghosh, Amitav. *The Great Derangement: Climate Change and the Unthinkable.* Chicago and London: The Chicago University Press, 2016.

Horowitz, Michael C. 'The Ethics and Morality of Robotic Warfare: Assessing The Debate Over Autonomous Weapons'. *Daedalus.* Vol. 145, No. 4, 2016, pp. 25–36.

Joy, Bill. 'Why the Future Doesn't Need Us'. *Wired.* April 1, 2000. Retrieved January 25, 2018, from https://www.wired.com/2000/04/joy-2/.

Keane, Daniel. 'Philosopher David Chalmers on Consciousness, the Hard Problem and the Nature of Reality'. *ABC News.* July 7, 2017. Retrieved November 11, 2017, from http://www.abc.net.au/news/2017-07-07/david-chalmers-and-the-puzzle-of-consciousness/8679884.

Koch, Christof. 'When Does Consciousness Arise in Human Babies?' *Scientific American.* September 1, 2009. Retrieved October 7, 2017, from https://www.scientificamerican.com/article/when-does-consciousness-arise/.

Koch, Christof, and Tononi, Giulio. 'Can Machines Be Conscious'. *IEEE Spectrum.* June 1, 2008. Retrieved October 9, 2017, from https://spectrum.ieee.org/biomedical/imaging/can-machines-be-conscious.

Lagercrantz, Hugo, and Changeux, Jean-Pierre. 'The Emergence of Human Consciousness: From Fetal to Neonatal Life'. *Paediatric Research.* Vol. 65, 2009, pp. 255–260.

McCauley, Lee. 'The Frankenstein Complex and Asimov's Three Laws', Association for the Advancement of Artificial Intelligence, 2007. Retrieved November 12, 2017, from https://www.aaai.org/Papers/Workshops/2007/WS-07-07/WS07-07-003.pdf.

Morton, Timothy. *Humankind: Solidarity with Nonhuman People*. London: Verso, 2017.

Regalado, Antonio. 'What It Will Take for Computers to Be Conscious'. *MIT Technology Review*. October 2, 2014. Retrieved November 12, 2018, from https://www.technologyreview.com/s/531146/what-it-will-take-for-computers-to-be-conscious/.

Reichardt, Jasia. *Robots: Fact, Fiction and Prediction*. London: Thames and Hudson, 1978.

Searle, John. 'Consciousness'. *Annual Review of Neuroscience*. Vol. 23, 2000, pp. 557–578.

Sloman, Aaron. 'Why Asimov's Three Laws of Robotics are Unethical'. 2006. Retrieved October 30, 2017, from http://www.cs.bham.ac.uk/research/projects/cogaff/misc/asimov-three-laws.html.

Turkle, Sherry. *Life on the Screen: Identity in the Age of the Internet*. New York: Simon and Schuster, 1995.

Vyverberg, Henry. *Human Nature, Cultural Diversity, and the French Enlightenment*. New York and Oxford: Oxford University Press, 1989.

Website

University of Cambridge. 'On the Origin of (Robot) Species', Research, 2015. Retrieved December 13, 2017, from http://www.cam.ac.uk/research/news/on-the-origin-of-robot-species.

CHAPTER 4

Imagining a Robot Death

Abstract This chapter examines the portrayal of robot deaths in popular culture. The portrayal of robot deaths in film and television allows for a broader understanding of the manner in which we view and treat the phenomenon of death as something inherently biological. This chapter also investigates the manner in which we employ language to further separate humans from machines. Popular culture is particularly useful in offering an alternative perspective when discussing the notion of machine mortality, focusing more on behaviour, rather than biology. Furthermore, this chapter discusses the extent to which a robot could be considered a divine figure.

Keywords Robots · Death · Science fiction · Clones · Language Suffering

In one of the units that I teach, we have a week on the 'ethical turn', and in class, we show a clip from an episode of Battlestar Gallactica, 'A Measure of Salvation'. The humans in the episode uncover the means through which to destroy the artificial Cylon race, created by humans and bent on human destruction. The ethical dilemma in the episode is whether or not the humans should actually go ahead with their plan to destroy the entire race of Cylons. On the one hand, some of the soldiers wish to secure their own survival, while on the other, it is argued that the act corresponds to genocide.

© The Author(s) 2018
S. Lyons, *Death and the Machine*,
https://doi.org/10.1007/978-981-13-0335-7_4

Each year when we've done this activity, we receive the same response from students about what they would do: the majority see genocide as morally justifiable to ensure the survival of humanity. And every year about two students out of thirty argue that exterminating the robot race is morally unacceptable. The last time I asked my student this question, the majority of students argued against eliminating the Cylons on the grounds that it was morally unjustifiable, even if it threatened the survival of the human species.

Such discussions give curious insight into the attitudes people have towards the existential nature of a non-living machine. In previous years, more students agreed with the character Lee Adama, who maintains that because the Cylons are not human, there is no ethical quandary. In many ways, the response was unsurprising. Yet the gradual change in attitudes attests the growing status that machines have in a post-human context. Advancing science and more sophisticated technology is not the only reason for this. Representations of machines and the non-human in popular culture have an underestimated role in opening up a crucial dialogue on the nature of existence, challenging the conventional approach to seeing human beings as a superior species and the only one worthy of life.

The Robot's Fear of Death

As discussed in the second chapter, the fear of death is a common and understandable trait of humanity. At present, humanoid robots that have been created in real life do not express a fear of death as we understand it, and this is what most notably differentiates humans and robots from each other. As Matt Damon's character Dr. Mann states in *Interstellar*, robots do not improvise well because 'you cannot program a fear of death'. The fear of death is not a programmable element, but an innate one, based on the biological inevitability of death. And since robots are often considered unable to die in a biological sense, their potential fears of death are often dismissed as either irrational or imaginary.

Despite their apparent inability to die, the robot's fear of death has continuously been portrayed throughout science fiction films and texts. Yet it is a death that does not carry the same weight, significance or consideration as a biological death. This is part of what makes the robot death both so poignant and so tragic; the demise occurs but without being considered real or authentic, further plaguing the non-human character for whom death remains an occurrence all the same.

The dilemma in the idea of a robot death is famously explored in Isaac Asimov's *The Bicentennial Man*, in which a robot undergoes surgery to become a human precisely in order to die. The robot, Andrew Martin, is continuously rejected in his pursuit to be considered human due to his immortality.

Asimov's text is one of the most useful in the discussion of a robot death, since the lack of mortality is automatically used to negate the possibility of being considered human, once again linking the essence of humanity to its mortality. By the story's end, Andrew succumbs to death, and is recognised as a human by the World Legislature. Rather than fearing death, Andrew welcomes it as a marker of his humanity.

Possibly the most notable example of a popular culture work in which a robot's fear of death is a major plot-point that actually propels the storyline is Ridley Scott's *Blade Runner* (1982), based on Philip K. Dick's 1961 novel *Do Androids Dream of Electric Sheep*. In the film, Deckard (Harrison Ford) is tasked with tracking down and 'retiring' three replicants including Roy Batty (Rutger Hauer), Leon (Brion James) and Pris (Darryl Hannah), humanoid robots who have rebelled against their makers and murder others who disrupt their goal.

In contrast to the film, originally the replicants were, according to Dick, 'essentially less-than-human entities' (Sammon 1996: 285). Instead, they were 'deplorable', 'cruel', 'cold' and 'heartless'. He argued that 'they have no empathy', and that they 'don't care about what happens to other creatures'. As Steve Rose argues, Ridley Scott's film 'turned it around, somewhat. Far from being a deplorable, heartless machine, Rutger Hauer's chief replicant, supposedly the baddie, develops empathy for the cop trying to kill him. Replicants were the superior beings' (Rose 2017).

This deviation from the original manner in which replicants were conceived is particularly useful in showing how attitudes regarding robots were already beginning to change when the original *Blade Runner* was being made. In 1982, the second international conference on artificial intelligence was held, suggesting that as more discussions on artificial intelligence were occurring, the attitudes regarding the robot were gradually changing too.

Blade Runner's take on the plot was thus useful in reframing notions of humanity. As Rose points out, 'Human status was no longer a matter of biological or genetic fact. You couldn't trust your memories either— they could just be implants. So how do any of us know we are human?'

Blade Runner was one of the first films to question the entitled nature of being human; it undermined the presumption that we could depend on any one factor—biological or psychological—to validate our humanity. In the original film, replicants were designed with a lifespan of only four years, yet Batty helms an attack on his creators in order to attain a larger lifespan. He puts it clearly and bluntly to his creator, Tyrell: 'I want more life, fucker!' In an effort to prolong his life, Batty murders Tyrell and attempts to kill Deckard.

Although all three replicants are portrayed as antagonists throughout the film, killing any character who inhibits their desire for more life, their actions register as desperate acts stemming from an intense fear of death. Roy Batty, in particular, expresses a tremendous fear of death, which propels his actions throughout the film. The replicants, unsurprisingly, have a strong connection to life due to their incredibly short lifespans. As Mark Rowlands describes the replicants: 'They are, or certainly seem to be, emotionally and intellectually sensitive creatures, with a clear sense of their own mortality, and a corresponding fear of death' (2005: 235).

As discussed in the second chapter, a strong awareness of death, as well as death itself, appears fundamentally human. The replicants in *Blade Runner*, having only a lifespan of four years, have a hyper-awareness of their technological mortality, and therefore could be understood as more human than their human counterparts due precisely to their transience. Thus not only is death a universal theme, but one that is shared by man and machine alike, in this context, expanding the scope of death's philosophical implications.

In the final fight between Batty and Deckard, Batty decides to save Deckard's life at the last minute, and delivers perhaps the most famous death soliloquy in cinema:

> I've seen things you people wouldn't believe. Attack ships on fire off the shoulder of Orion. I watched C-beams glitter in the dark near the Tannhäuser Gate. All those moments will be lost in time, like tears in rain. Time to die.

It is in this moment that Roy Batty's drastic and horrific actions, while not entirely justifiable, are certainly understandable in the context of Roy's (non) life. Like other humans, Roy's desperation for life manifests itself in violent acts to ensure his longevity, as seen in innumerable films.

Rutger Hauer is known to have deviated from the script and improvised his final lines, and the monologue has since become one of the more famous in cinema.

Discussing Roy Batty's death scene, Rowlands describes it as 'the most moving death soliloquy in cinematic history' (235), one that captures 'the human (and also, apparently, the replicant) predicament' of our memories counting for precisely nothing.

Further, Rowlands posits that 'if we can work out the value of what death takes away, then we can, so the idea goes, work out the value of life' (237). Part of the value of life, in this respect, is the prolonged but temporary absence of our own death. Indeed, Rowlands looks at the manner in which life is viewed through the replicants that corresponds to our fear of death:

> Roy and his replicants wanted to avoid death because they wanted more life. And the underlying assumption here is that life is a good thing—another assumption that we, typically, share with Roy. Death is what takes away life. (236–237)

Relating this insight to the issues discussed in the second chapter, a fear of death is not merely aroused through the potential for pain that is associated with the process of dying. Death, quite simply, is that which deprives us of life, and by that understanding we perceive death as a negative phenomenon. While Epicurus suggests a fear of death is illogical since it is something we do not experience, our fears are certainly understandable in the context of seeing death as the absence of life, regardless of any lived experience of death (or lack thereof).

Yet if the replicants in *Blade Runner* were only confronted with the fearsome inevitability of death, then the film itself would not be offering much in the way of an original story, since a fear of death is at once universal and familiar. It is the fact that they are replicants confronting a non-death that proves even more disconcerting, since their death, which carries with it the same physical cessation of being, does not, however, carry with it the same biological or philosophical significance. Batty's death soliloquy suitably describes this predicament, that is, the apparent meaninglessness of their (very physical) death, as inconsequential as tears in the rain, more so than a human death because they have no biological demise undergirding their 'retirement'. So not only must Roy Batty and other replicants experience what certainly appears to be a physical death through the cessation of life, but their death is further disregarded, and is considered, in biological terms, inexistent, illegitimate, and inconsequential, in essence, a 'fake death'.

With the release of *Blade Runner 2049* (2017), the same question of what determines humanity resurfaced, particularly with the reappearance of Harrison Ford's Deckard, who, many assumed after the original film, was a replicant. The usual four-year lifespan is no longer in place for all replicants, and there is also no Voight-Kampff test to distinguish between humans and replicants. In the sequel, as Steve Rose points out, 'it is no longer possible to gauge who is human or not anymore', suggesting perhaps that the distinction had become redundant.

Ryan Gosling's K is, however, revealed to be a Nexus-9 replicant, whose job it is to track down rogue replicants and 'retire' them. When it is discovered that Deckard and Rachael (Sean Young) had a child after the events of the first film, undermining the assumption that replicants cannot bear children, K is ordered to cover it up and retire the child. Niander Wallace (Jared Letto), the CEO of the Wallace Corporation, intends to discover the secret behind replicant reproduction in order to aid his vision of interstellar colonisation.

The film delves into more discussions on the nature of humanity and death, particularly in regards to the dual processes of birth and death. After being ordered to kill the replicant child, a reluctant K muses that 'to be born is to have a soul', thereby aligning biological birth with consciousness. Yet he is also told by Freysa, the leader of the replicant freedom movement, that 'dying for a good cause is the most human thing we can do'.

A separation thus emerges between birth and death in regards to humanity; on the one hand we are presented with a scenario in which birth provides a biological basis on which to frame humanity. On the other hand, death and sacrifice are aspects that determine not one's ability to be human, but one's ability to be understood and considered as an ethical, sentient being. By the film's end, K dies after sustaining mortal injuries, suggesting that not only can replicants now die, but that they are capable of possessing certain characteristics that we steadfastly apply to humans. In fact, the sequel more strongly emphasises the humanly aspects of the robots over the 'real' human than the original film, showing that in the twenty-first century, robotic morality and the notion of ethical AI has become ever more persuasive.

In the same vein as *Blade Runner*, Stanley Kubrick's acclaimed film *2001: A Space Odyssey* (1968), similarly portrays not only the death of a robotic character, but one who is the primary antagonist of the film. HAL9000, the in-built robot on the ship *Discovery One* embodies society's fear of the disobeying robot rebelling against its creator and even causing death. Although said to be 'foolproof and incapable of error', HAL is seen to make a mistake reporting the failure of an antenna control device. When Mission Control advises that HAL is in error, HAL insists the issue was a result of human error. HAL ends up killing several of the astronauts, after which Dave Bowman, the surviving astronaut, decides to 'deactivate' HAL.

In a particularly unnerving scene, Dave delves into the chamber and slowly deactivates HAL, while the robot in turn protests in a detached, monotone voice against his technological death, reverting to his original programming and singing 'Daisy'. During his deactivation, HAL says: 'I'm afraid. I'm afraid, Dave. Dave, my mind is going. I can feel it. I can feel it. My mind is going. There is no question about it. I can feel it. I can feel it. I can feel it. I'm afraid'.

It is actually the monotone manner in which HAL protests that makes the scene so unnerving. Imagining the scene with HAL protesting in a frantic manner would not elicit the same response, as the scene's disconcerting resonance lies in HAL's detached helplessness as a robot. The viewer is made to feel both uncomfortable and sympathetic as HAL describes the distressing process of being robotically lobotomised.

The scene is also pivotal in its flipping of the human/robot binary, since HAL becomes more synonymous with a human through his very fallibility. William Indick makes the significant point that HAL is, in fact, 'more emotional than his human partners are' (2004: 139).

> He expresses concern and even fear about the mission and admits to "projecting" his own feelings, hinting that he not only as a conscious mind, but he has an unconscious as well. At the same moment, he makes his first error. The symbolism is unmistakable. HAL mentioned earlier with a sense of pride that no 9000-level computer has ever made an error. If the old adage is true, if "to err is human..." then HAL has shown himself to be more human than machine. Furthermore, he displays the all-too-human quality of defensiveness when he refuses to admit to the possibility that he may have made a mistake. (139)

This is what makes HAL's 'death' scene all the more unsettling, since his pleas for Dave's understanding and renewed fear of death strike a certain chord with those who see HAL as embodying more humanly traits than the humans aboard the ship, despite lacking the ability to ultimately defend himself when he is finally being 'deactivated'.

In his interpretation of the scene, Indick even goes so far as to suggest that it is the humans aboard the ship that exhibit less humanity than HAL: 'HAL's creator does not live up to his part of the adage: "...to forgive is divine"' (139). Instead of forgiving HAL, Indick notes, they disconnect him, despite being unaware that 'HAL has reached such a level of self-awareness that he now fears the loss of his consciousness as a human would fear death'. Indick posits that HAL's killing of Frank and the other astronauts is typically human in nature, borne out of self-defence and fear of culpability. He argues that 'with amazing speed, HAL has learned not only to value conscious life, but he has also learned when it is convenient to devalue it as well'.

By this same token, we have learned the extent to which a human takes on certain attributes that are uncharacteristically human; Dave's deactivation of HAL is at once cold and unemotional. It is HAL who we begin to feel for at this precise moment as he reverts to his most basic condition, an extension of the 'Sympathy for the Devil' trope in which the antagonist, through sudden vulnerability, is made a pitiable creature. HAL's actions, as Indick points out, are not too dissimilar from the actions of a human, and yet due to his robotic nature Dave (and presumably some of the audience) are inclined to link his actions to the cold savagery of robotics, failing to notice the same fallibility and behaviour in humans.

Semantics of a Robot Death

Popular culture serves as a platform on which to base ideals of artificial intelligence. While it offers speculations on the rights of robots, it also acts as a barrier between humanity and technology by framing robots and other non-humans in a distinct light through the use of semantics. Specifically, language is used to reframe the robot or non-human death in a manner to clearly distinguish between humanity and robots. In lieu of 'dying', robots and other non-human beings are 'retired', 'deactivated', 'regenerated', 'completed', or 'discorporated'. Language exists, therefore, to perpetuate existing distinctions between robots and humans, prioritising the existence of humans while essentially forbidding robots from achieving an 'authentic' death, despite experiencing the same fears of death as humans nonetheless. As Heidegger notes, 'the essential relation between death and language flashes up before us, but remains still unthought' (1982: 107).

As the aforementioned segment shows, neither HAL9000 nor Roy Batty are considered to have undergone an 'authentic', legitimate death, at least in the biological sense of the term. They are instead 'deactivated' and 'retired' respectively. They shut down in the same way that a computer does—seemingly without emotional resonance. The words describing their demise are clinical and detached, illustrating the same semantic detachment that we have formulated around the robot death.

In this manner, the semantics surrounding robot deaths in popular culture appears to be a way to achieve philosophical distance between the human and the robot; by not granting the robot with the description of death, the creators effectively contribute to its very dehumanisation, perhaps due to our innate fears not of the threat of robots to our lives, but of the threat they pose to our usually stable definitions of humanity. Once a robot is granted the same ability to 'die', we offer an unnerving parallel between humanity and death that previously remained unambiguous.

The connection between language and death is explored in *Brain Death and Disorders of Consciousness* (2004). Looking at the manner in which different languages approach the notion of death, Shewmon and Shewmon argue that 'death concepts and the whole death debate can be influenced by language: namely, the distinction that many languages, but not English, make between human and non-human death' (103).

They note that in Poland, there are two nouns for death: *śmierć* is used in everyday speech and relates most accurately to the English form of death, while *zgon* means 'death of a person' and is more formal and medical. The Polish language also has two separate words for 'to die'; while *umrzeć* is used exclusively for humans, *zdechnąć* is used in reference to animals or 'derogatorily in reference to humans' (103). The German language similarly separates human and non-human death, where *sterben* applies strictly to humans, verenden refers to the death of animals, and eingehen relates to the death of plants and animals.

Interestingly, the 'death-words' in Hindi, Shewmon and Shewmon explain, 'apply equally to humans and animals, but not to plants' (103–104). In Hindi, a plant only withers, but does not die. 'Thus', they argue, 'the Hindi language both reflects and reinforces the Hindi belief in reincarnation among *sentient* forms of life' (104, emphasis mine).

Therefore sentience becomes a key factor in determining the manner in which language is used in regards to death, and may explain why popular culture has so many varied words to describe a robot's demise.

Substituting the word 'death' is not too uncommon in science fiction; in Robert Heinlein's novel *Stranger in a Strange Land* (1961), for example, the concept of death is replaced with 'discorporation', the Martian term for death. It is more of a spiritual term that refers to a person who chooses to leave their body. In other situations, however, the non-human has no choice. In the television series *Doctor Who*, the Time Lord—an immortal being from the planet Gallifrey—never dies, but is destined to be regenerated over and over again, assuming a new form once the old Time Lord begins to deteriorate.

The Tenth Doctor, played by David Tennant, was one of the more popular doctors in the series (if not the most popular), and his 'death' scene was equally compelling. Tennant's incredibly emotional demise in 'The End of Time' (2009–2010) has been voted one of the saddest deaths in modern television. In Whitney Jefferson's Buzzfeed list of 30 Saddest Television Deaths, she includes Tennant's Doctor as an honourable mention, noting that '*technically* David Tennant's character on Doctor Who regenerated into the Eleventh Doctor and didn't straight-up die. Regardless, it still felt like a TV death because it was terribly sad'.

After having his regeneration accelerated, the tenth Doctor responds with intense anger and frustration, before begrudgingly accepting his imminent death. But just before he regenerates, the tenth Doctor's fear is clear and palpable. His fearful plea: 'I don't want to go', right the moment before he begins regenerating, registers especially poignantly with a society that often expresses a fear of death, particularly an untimely one. As with Roy Batty and HAL9000, the tenth Doctor expresses fear of death despite his apparent non-human status and the fact that his death is not considered an actual death, but is classified only as a 'regeneration'. The Doctor is immortal after all, and yet the changing face of the entity corresponds to a repeated loss of life.

Kristine Larsen's chapter 'Everything Dies: The Message of Mortality in the Ecclestone and Tennant Years' (2013) provides a useful critique of the place of mortality in *Doctor Who*, in which death is often 'an uncredited guest star' (157). *Doctor Who* operates, Larsen explains, as a broader metaphor for the unwillingness to accept the inevitability of death:

Death is a natural part of life, and the untimely death of any individual or species is to be avoided at all costs, and lamented where inevitable. However, accepting this inevitability is often easier said than done, both in the primary world and in the universe of Doctor Who. In both the televised episodes and tie-in novels of the ninth and tenth incarnations of the Doctor (portrayed by Christopher Eccleston and David Tennant, respectively), we see this bitter lesson played over and over again, as otherwise intelligent creatures—be they Humans, Daleks, Gappa, and even (one might say especially) Time Lords—refuse to swallow this bitter pill. (157–158)

The Time Lord's immortality notwithstanding, the process of regeneration forces us to consider our own mortality. As Larsen notes, 'the Doctor stumbles back to the TARDIS, resisting his regeneration to the very last moment' (171). Indeed, his last words are a desperate, very human appeal against not just death, but the non-being that goes along with death. For while the Doctor is immortal, the eleventh Doctor (Matt Smith) takes over as the new incarnation of the Doctor, mirroring the process of death. As Larsen writes:

> The tenth Doctor fights against his own death not only because of his own attachment to that incarnation, but because after living in his various forms for nine centuries, he understands how precious life truly is, in all its forms. While death cannot be defeated, it can sometimes be sidestepped for the time being. (172)

Like the replicants, individual *incarnations* of the Time Lord have a comparatively short lifespan (although the actual Time Lord can live for hundreds if not thousands of years). With the exception of the immensely popular Tom Baker, who played the role for almost seven years, the active period of each incarnation of the Time Lord varies, with Eccleston's incarnation lasting for three months, in comparison to Tennant, who played the character for six years.

Much discussion has circulated around whether or not the Doctor becomes a new person after regeneration, a topic that has significant implications for the understanding of how death works. Since the Doctor appears to become an entirely different being, with his or her unique physical and character attributes, then regeneration operates very much like a death. Yet the new Doctor possesses all the memories of his previous incarnations, making the process of regeneration distinct from death at the same time. As Justin Andress asks: 'What effect does regeneration have on the soul of a being who finds himself housed in a completely different shell at the end of cataclysmic trauma? Can he possibly be the same person, or is he a new person, born as a result of the Doctor's previous horrors?' (2016). Andress points out that the tenth Doctor's regeneration distinguished itself completely from all previous ones due to his emotional plea:

> Before the tenth Doctor, no other incarnation had protested his regeneration. Fan theory states that the tenth Doctor's unusual fear is a sign that he's expecting his own final death, not another regeneration. That fear of the true unknown is what causes his ultimate reluctance. However, isn't the tenth Doctor's fear essentially well-founded? Once he regenerates into Matt Smith, isn't Tennant essentially gone forever (well, at least until the 50th anniversary special)? (2016)

Andress alludes to the three primary aspects of identity as outlined by philosopher Michael Hand: character, physicality and memory. While the Doctor changes in terms of personality and appearance with each regeneration, Andress notes that 'things get a little stickier when we get to his memory, as the Doctor *does* retain his memories of past events from body to body. Does memory alone a person make?'

Michael Hand discusses the different approaches to the death and regeneration question in *Doctor Who*, noting that different Doctors provoke different ideas of what the regeneration entails. He notes that the second Doctor 'compares his regeneration from the first to the metamorphosis of caterpillars into butterflies, implying an unbroken continuation of life' (2011: 217). Yet the regeneration of the seventh Doctor into the eighth, he argues, 'gives powerful support to the death hypothesis (217)'.

After the seventh Doctor is mortally shot in the chest during a gun battle, he is pronounced dead in a hospital, but regenerates into the eighth Doctor three hours later in the morgue. He explains to the cardiologist, Dr. Grace Holloway, that he had been dead too long, with the anaesthetic almost destroying the 'regenerative process'. This explanation, Hand argues, 'not only confirms that the Doctor was indeed dead for the three plus hours prior to his regeneration, but also clearly implies that regeneration *always* involves death, albeit usually for a shorter period of time' (217).

Hand aligns regeneration to 'a literal form of resurrection', in which 'the Doctor comes back from the dead each time he regenerates' (217). But he notes that the relevance of regeneration in this respect has broader philosophical implications:

> What's important about regeneration, for our present purposes, is what it tells us about how much change a person can undergo while still remaining the same person. Whether the radical transformation of the regenerative process involves an actual dying and rising, or just something analogous to one, is by the by. (217)

Doctor Who is a prime example of both the non-human's fear of death and the semantics involved in the death of a non-human; the extent to which each incarnation of the Doctor retains the same sense of self (while evidently appearing different), as well as the extent to which regeneration unequivocally implies death, is not at all conclusive. But as Hand explains, there is certainly a sense that the processes of both regeneration and death are significantly interlinked in their production of something new in resurrection. This would therefore make Tennant's fearful state right before his own regeneration both understandable and relatable, since even if each subsequent Doctor retains memories of their past selves, they are always in some sense different, and not just physically.

As Shewmon and Shewmon's aforementioned work suggests about the ability for language to create various types and understandings of death, so too does *Doctor Who* operate in this way, where 'regeneration' implies another form of death that is similar but distinct from a human death, and it is in this characteristic that *Doctor Who* is philosophically significant.

Other works which focus on the ambiguous relationship between death and the non-human through semantics include Kazuo Ishiguro's acclaimed work *Never Let Me Go* (2005), which focuses on the fictional private school of Hailsham. It is eventually revealed, primarily through the protagonist's—Katy's—flashbacks, that the children are, in fact, clones, engineered purposefully for their organs as substitutes for real humans. While at school, the children engage in art, music and literature, bond with each other, and even fall in love. Some are able to become carers, such as Katy, while others, such as Katy's friend Ruth, exist specifically and purposefully as organ donors for humans. The clones are expected to eventually give up all of their vital organs, until they 'complete', another word used to denote a particular kind of non-human death. The clone is not seen to die, as such, but is completed in their task once their reason for being is finished.

In one respect, *Never Let Me Go* operates as the embodiment of society's awareness and subsequent fears of our eventual death; just as the clones gradually come to understand their place in life and imminent death, before adjusting to its realities, so too do humans struggle to accept that of which they have come to be aware. And yet the clones' sole purpose is to die, to serve other humans. Their life, therefore, is inextricably bound up in their death, more so than any other being.

In her analysis of the book in regards to mortality, Virginia Yeung posits that 'in many stories with a sci-fi touch or dystopian element, scientific terms are used to create a sense of authority or an illusion of reality in the narrative' (2017: 2). However, she argues that this is not the case for *Never Let Me Go*, in which simple words such as 'donors', 'carers' and 'guardians' are used to describe characters. And she argues that this has the function of alluding to the phenomenon of death without actually treating it as such:

> Euphemisms in the novel have a dual function of masking the enterprise of cloning as well as expressing death-related notions. Echoing the way human beings talk about death and its related concepts, positive-sounding words are used in the story to refer to such ideas. 'Donation' means enforced extraction of vital organs, and the clones 'complete' or die after the donations. Such euphemisms are closely linked to the notion of death because cloning is a science born out of human beings' wish to exercise control over their mortality. (2)

Indeed, the presence of clones in the novel both connects and distances humans in regards to death; the clones are a metaphorical extension of human beings in the same way that replicants are, appearing human but encountering drastic limitations in their ability to be deemed human, specifically but not exclusively through the element of death.

The fact that the clones are described as 'something troubling and strange' is yet another indicator that we wish to separate the human from the non-human, particularly in regards to death. If Ishiguro simply rendered the demise of his clones as a 'death', then they would be more closely aligned with humans, acknowledging a similarity between the clone and the human, a fact which would be itself troubling and strange for certain people who value the human life above all else.

The use of the death-related concept 'complete', like the words regenerate and retirement, therefore, becomes a hierarchical method through which the superiority of humankind is reinforced, where the human is valued for its naturalness, reiterating the notion that only humans can ever experience a valid death. As Yeung writes, 'mortality can be interpreted as a privilege of humankind, a symbol of its superiority in being the only species endowed with an intellectual and emotional dimension' (4). Through this superiority, moreover, the non-human becomes doubly disadvantaged, for not only must the clones succumb to an awful fate, but their lack of biological humanity appears to negate their ability to truly die, something which would ordinarily grant their lives unquestionable meaning. As Yeung argues, 'the clones suffer a much crueller fate than human beings', not only because they operate in servitude to actual humans, but because they are robbed of a valid death in their non-humanity, despite suffering all the same. This is what makes the novel so disheartening; we are inclined to sympathise with the characters, even mourn them, despite knowing that they are not human. It is in their non-humanity that our sympathies are intensified, as they are for other helpless, non-human beings such as animals.

The despairing element of the novel however creates a refuge from the non-biological death issue; in caring for these characters, Ishiguro allows readers the possibility to imagine and potentially accept a non-human's death to be as real and genuine as a human's. Like *The Bicentennial Man, Blade Runner, 2001: A Space Odyssey* and *Doctor Who*, all of which similarly contain non-human characters who encounter and fear death, *Never Let Me Go* humanises the non-human specifically through the lens of death. The characters are partially modelled on humans, whether through error, as seen with HAL, anger and violence as seen with *Blade Runner*, fear in *Doctor Who*, or a morbid but realistic passivity as seen with *Never Let Me Go*. As Yeung explains, the novel 'leads us to contemplate our own existence [...] by making the characters totally passive' (4). For both Yeung and Ishiguro, death is generally accepted somewhat passively by humans, at least in the long term. Even if we express fear, we do not necessarily act out our fears in any sort of physical way as we might expect, making the clones' passivity in *Never Let Me Go* more understandable and relatable than we may initially realise.

The threat of death is, as Ernest Becker's earlier sentiments attest, something that is maintained but not on an entirely conscious level. Because of the assumed timespan between birth and death, we register its threat, but also temporarily cast it aside because of its apparent distance from our lived experiences. It is, in a sense, both present and absent; present on a biological level, but absent on a conscious one. But the clones also accept their reality because they ultimately have no choice, just as with humans. As Yeung notes, 'human beings embrace the notion of death because they know their physical limitations' (5).

Language provides a safe distance between robots and humans, between the human and non-human. In developing substitutes for the word and concept of death, humans are privileged in the life-death equation.

FUNCTIONALISM AND THE NON-BIOLOGICAL HUMAN

If we consider the actual behaviour of many of the non-human characters in popular culture who are confronted with the prospect of death, then we can start to reformulate ideas of what constitutes 'humanity'. In discussing the emphasis on one's behaviour, rather than their existential make-up, it is useful here to discuss the philosophical theory of functionalism, that is, looking at a particular being's mental status as dependent on its function, not on its internal composition. For functionalists, a being's mental state is not determined by its 'biological substrate' alone, but is shaped by the social structure. In other words, it is behaviour which determines the validity of a person's being, rather than their biological construction.

Functionalism 'studied the mind in terms of its function in the adaptation of an individual to his environment' and 'stressed the personal qualities of the individual mind' (Ebong and Bassey 1995: 22). Or, as Dennett argues, for a functionalist, 'it makes no difference whether a system is made of organic molecules or silicon, so long as it does the same job. Artificial hearts don't have to be made of organic tissue, and neither do artificial brains—at least in principle' (1993: 31). We can expand this line of thinking to a theory that accommodates the idea that a being can be judged as an ethical being entity not by its biological substrate, but by how well it functions morally. Just as an artificial heart can, in theory, support a robot, an organic heart does not automatically validate or denote an ethical human, as the entirety of human history exemplifies.

In this way, while functionalism does not tell us anything empirical about the inner constructions of the mind, its move away from biological determinism is useful in a discussion of robot life, since we can view behaviour as a more reliable indicator of an ethical being.

Although the robot has often been portrayed in an antagonistic manner, such as Roy Batty and HAL9000, more recently popular culture has represented robots not merely in a benevolent light, as with *The Bicentennial Man* or *Wall-E*, but in a distinctly philosophical manner through notions of suffering and redemption.

AMC's *Westworld* best exemplifies the robot's trajectory from robotics to humanity, focusing on the link between a robot's behaviour and their capacity to be 'more human than human'. Notably, the actual humans in *Westworld* are portrayed as callous, dismissive, and abhorrent, raping and abusing the robots of the theme park. But rather than projecting the robot hosts in merely a submissive or even a benevolent role, the robots are much more nuanced, complex creations. They do not merely seek to do good, but actually, in their strive for humanity, commit acts that are similarly questionable. This is what makes *Westworld* such a crucial and useful artefact of discussion.

Based on the 1974 film of the same name, *Westworld* centres on an Eighteenth-century Western-themed amusement park, in which wealthy human guests pay $10,000 a day to tour the park and engage with its robotic hosts, many of whom are subjected to brutal, submissive roles. There solely to acquiesce to the wealthy guests, the robotic hosts have their memories wiped every day, forgetting each and every savage occurrence, until a mechanical glitch enables the robots to question their realities. As many of the robots, including Dorothy Abernathy and Maeve, gradually become more aware of their predicament, the park's engineers attempt to suppress their growing sentience, with varying success.

Bound by certain regulations that mirror Asimov's Three Laws of Robotics, the hosts are not wilfully or physically able to kill a human. By the last episode of the first season, however, the host Dorothy shoots and kills the park's founder, Dr. Ford, culminating in a mass panic.

The robots, in their striving for consciousness, are continually subjected to suffering, whether through actual, physical abuse, or through psychological abuse due to having their memories wiped, or being forced to repeat the same exact storyline every day, forever controlled by their creators. This sinister memory loss is a significant factor that robs the robots of their potential for consciousness.

Yet in and through their suffering, the robots are seen to be affirming their humanity, projecting humanity as a concept one must *earn*, rather than something that is automatically gained at birth. Their suffering determines their humanity, and they become, by way of struggle, more human than the actual humans in *Westworld* for whom humanity is strictly a biological phenomenon. As the Man in Black himself states in the episode 'Chestnut', 'When you're suffering, that's when you're most real'.

A number of philosophers have previously linked the concept of humanity to the presence of struggle or suffering. Friedrich Nietzsche is one of the main proponents of philosophical suffering, in which he aligns the greatness of humanity to humankind's emergence through suffering. In *Beyond Good and Evil*, he proclaims:

> The discipline of suffering, of great suffering—do you not know that only this discipline has created all enchantments of man so far? That tension of the soul in unhappiness which cultivates its strength, its shudders face to face with great ruin, its inventiveness and courage in enduring, persevering, interpreting, and exploiting suffering, and whatever has been granted to it of profundity, secret, mask, spirit, cunning, greatness—was it not granted to it through suffering, through the discipline of great suffering? (1989: 154)

The endurance of the robotic hosts, in spite of or perhaps *due* to their suffering, affirms their potential for humanity, or for sentience, and radically alters the dimensions and definitions of humanity, offering the notion that behaviour, rather than biology, may determine one's capacity to be considered truly human in the moral sense.

If we discuss the notion of humanity based on Aristotle's well-known theories of human excellence, then the argument that robots could be understood as more human than human becomes more persuasive. The actions of the humans in Westworld—the rapes that both the guests and engineers commit, the gleeful murders in which they partake—directly confront and undermine Aristotle's ideals of humanity. One may be more inclined to accept the robots as potentially ideal figures through their desperate struggle to attain consciousness, a phenomenon that humans themselves take for granted.

Aristotle's theory of human excellence is based on the opposing elements of vice and virtue. When discussing virtues in his *Nicomachean Ethics*, Aristotle puts forth the argument that humans must avoid three types of character: 'vice, incontinence and brutality' (1869: 209). In contrast, one must act with virtue in comparison to vice, and with self-restraint in comparison to incontinence. In regards to brutality, Aristotle notes that 'what would seem to be most fittingly opposed to brutality is that virtue which *transcends the human*. Indeed, Aristotle aligns this with a sense of godliness, since, for him, the 'excellence of a god is something to be held in higher honour than any human virtue'. By that same token, Aristotle speaks of 'the evil nature of a beast' which is 'something specifically distinct from any form of vice'.

While Aristotle notes that it is rare or difficult to come by a human of 'godlike nature' (210), he also acknowledges that such evilness is equally rare, but nevertheless in existence. He writes that such evil is found 'among savages', 'applied to those whose vice is *worse than human*'.

If one were to apply Aristotle's views on human excellence to the portrayal of robots in popular culture, it could be said that his description of that which *transcends the human* could inadvertently refer or apply to robots themselves. For Aristotle, the excellence of a god is distinct from the excellence of a human, and exceeds 'any human virtue'. In this sense it is possible that that which exceeds human excellence is a robot that resembles a human but possesses certain virtuous characteristics that exceed humanity. Being that a god is both human-like in appearance but something more than human, the human-like robot conforms to certain notions of idolatry.

Although religion and robotics rarely convergence, Masahiro Mori strongly advocated the notion that a robot could become a god, a view he expressed at length in his underrated work *The Buddha in the Robot* (1974). In this work, Mori argues that just as there is what he calls the 'buddha-nature' in humans, animals and insects, 'there must also be a buddha-nature in the machines and robots that my colleagues and I make' (1981: 174). Mori's assertion is crucial in illustrating a shift in perception regarding the fusion of the natural and the synthetic, and Mori's attitude is notably progressive in acknowledging various forms of life that do not conform to certain biological constraints of life.

In valuing the robot life, Mori offers some useful words of wisdom: 'The first point in locating the buddha-nature is to quit valuing only that which we find convenient and denigrating that which we do not find convenient. Unless we adopt a broader sense of values, we will not be able to see that the buddha-nature is present in all things' (175).

Machines are certainly an inconvenient being when it comes to designating the value of life. But Mori's views attest to the notion that machines may invariably be capable of attaining some semblance of sentience beyond even the capacity of the biological human, becoming, in effect, a non-biological human.

Machines, then, will never be human in a biological sense; they can, of course, be seen as organic matter, but not in a way that makes them the same as a human. But this fact does not therefore negate their capability of being considered an ethical being. In fact, as both this chapter and the previous chapters point out, robots can potentially behave in ways that transcend human morality. What this means, then, is that biology and morality are not mutually exclusive, because being human does not automatically signify morality. The ability for a robot to be sentient, therefore, removes biology from the equation when we discuss the behaviour of humans. If humans are not the only beings that can display sentience and mortality, then the biological essentialism with which we so often approach life becomes unstable.

REFERENCES

Andress, Justin. 'What Happens to the Doctor When He Regenerates?' *Inverse*. April 20, 2016. Retrieved November 13, 2017, from https://www.inverse.com/article/14571-what-exactly-happens-to-the-doctor-when-he-regenerates.

Aristotle. *The Nicomachean Ethics of Aristotle*. London: Longman, 1869.

Dennett, Daniel. *Consciousness Explained*. London: Penguin, 1993.

Ebong, Maurice, and Bassey, Bassey J. *Environmental Perception and Human Behaviour*. Mushin: Macmillan Nigeria Publishers, 1995.

Hand, Michael. 'Regeneration and Resurrection'. *Doctor Who and Philosophy: Bigger on the Inside*. Lewis, Courtland and Smithka, Paula (eds.). Chicago and La Salle: Popular Culture and Philosophy, Open Court, 2011, pp. 213–224.

Heidegger, Martin. *On the Way to Language*. New York: Harper and Row Publishers, 1982.

Indick, William. *Movies and the Mind: Theories of the Great Psychoanalysts Applied to Film*. Jefferson: McFarland and Company, 2004.

Larsen, Kristine. 'Everything Dies: The Message of Mortality in the Eccleston and Tennant Years'. *Doctor Who in Time and Space: Essays on Themes, Characters, History and Fandom, 1963–2012*. Leitch, Gillian I. (ed.). Jefferson: McFarland and Company, 2013, pp. 157–174.

Mori, Masahiro. *The Buddha in the Robot*. Tokyo: Kōsei Publishing, 1981.

Nietzsche, Friedrich. *On the Genealogy of Morals and Ecce Homo*. New York: Vintage Books, 1989.

Rose, Steve. '"I've Seen Things You People Wouldn't Believe": What Blade Runner 2049's Dystopia Tells Us About 2017'. *The Guardian*. October 6, 2017. Retrieved October 12, 2017, from https://www.theguardian.com/film/2017/oct/06/blade-runner-2049-dystopian-vision-seen-things-wouldntbelieve.

Rowlands, Mark. *The Philosopher at the End of the Universe: Philosophy Explained Through Science Fiction Films*. London: Ebury Press, 2005.

Sammon, Paul M. *Future Noir: The Making of Blade Runner*. New York: Harper Paperbacks, 1996.

Shewmon, D. Alan, and Shewmon, Elisabeth Seitz. 'The Semiotics of Death and Its Medical Implications'. *Brain Death and Disorders of Consciousness*. Machado, Calixto and Shewmon, D. Alan (eds.). Advances in Experimental Medicine and Biology. Volume 550, 2004, pp. 89–114.

Yeung, Virginia. 'Mortality and Memory in Kazuo Ishiguro's *Never Let Me Go*'. *Transnational Literature*. Vol. 9, No. 2, May 2017, pp. 1–13.

CHAPTER 5

Conclusion: Death Beyond Biology

Abstract In this concluding chapter, I finalise the debate regarding the manner in which society has viewed itself in a superior manner in regards to life and death. Using Deleuze's philosophy, I argue how robots, in their future form, can be seen as what Deleuze calls a 'people-to-come', ushering in a new understanding a ways of being and ways of dying that do not abide by or conform to a rigid, biological constraint. I also argue how consciousness does not necessarily hold the same importance it once did in the economy of life, while death can be seen more as a moral phenomenon, rather than an intrinsically biological one.

Keywords Death · Humanism · Culture · Consciousness · Biology

Descartes' most famous and enduring maxim, 'I think, therefore I am' no longer commands the same influence it once did in the area of evolving humanity. What determines an essence of 'being' remains ambiguous and malleable, though many scholars and philosophers have still attempted to reduce humanity or, more broadly, 'life', to a particular set of conditions, which more often than not conform to certain biological constraints that prohibit other ways of being. But if consciousness no longer defines life, then neither does death, rendering the 'I die, therefore I am' alternative insufficient. Death, as this book has shown, no longer defines us as humans, but humanity still goes to great pains to defend its right to an essential, superior human nature, if not through

© The Author(s) 2018
S. Lyons, *Death and the Machine*,
https://doi.org/10.1007/978-981-13-0335-7_5

death, than through other phenomena. But too much has changed to allow this biological essentialism to endure. Different and conflicting ways of being, and of being alive, proliferate. The potential for a robot to be considered both a living and dying species is becoming more and more possible. And as more humans attempt to defy the once-inevitable fate of death, death itself has claimed a renewed sense of importance in determining different kinds of life that go beyond the human, and the organic.

It seems doubtful, however, that society would ever collectively accommodate or accept a re-evaluation of the notion of biological death that includes or permits a non-human, such as a machine. This kind of anxiety—acutely expressed in popular culture—stems from an enduring humanist approach to existence, in which the human claims sovereignty not just in ecological or biological circumstances, but in social and cultural ones as well. Because although social characteristics are not unique to humanity—various animals are known to possess characteristics which we would otherwise acknowledge as social and cultural—humans have nevertheless adopted the view that they are uniquely social and cultural, a line of thinking they have used to support their apparent superiority.

Humans developed science, law, art, music, literature, education, politics and philosophy. Because of the manner in which humanity developed into more of a cultured animal, we similarly ascribed a more significant value onto a human death than any other kind of death, including both living and non-living beings. An animal's death, a tree being cut down, or a machine being destroyed are not given the same sense of significance as a human's cessation of life. And this is despite the fact that not all humans are valued in the same way, and that not all humans possess or enact behaviour that we would consider living up to certain ideals of humanity.

Too often society underplays the similarities between humans and other living beings in the animal kingdom, despite Darwin, like Freud, radically re-establishing a link between humanity and the animal world that had been rejected by the social and scientific conventions of their time. It seems that despite this development, humanism retains its sway despite obvious similarities between both animals.

The existence of culture, for example, is not a phenomenon uniquely affiliated with humanity alone. Whales have culture; they have music and complex communication. Chimpanzees are social animals, ones which, as we already know, share 98.5% of human genes. And vampire bats are known to possess reciprocal altruism. Humans didn't invent the concept of culture or civility. In many ways, then, culture might therefore be itself a product of biology, of nature, rather than something distinct from nature. What makes humanity special or unique, therefore, cannot necessarily be found within the biological world and by comparing human culture and achievement with the animal world, because humans are not too distinct from other creatures in the animal kingdom. We are, as AC Grayling (2013) reminds us, fundamentally part of nature (even sharing 60% of our genes with tomatoes). Friedrich Nietzsche did observe differences, however, noting that the human being is 'more sick, uncertain, changeable, indeterminate than any other animal', calling the human 'the sick animal', 'wrestling with animals, nature and gods for ultimate domination' (121).

But humans cannot rest on their differences from animals to explain their apparent superiority. This either means that humanity's superiority needs to be found elsewhere, or, more likely, that the superiority with which humans have obstinately functioned does not, in fact, exist. Yet society continually seeks the answer of what makes humans special, and what defines human nature, or humankind. If the answer cannot be found in the biological world, then the rising technological world may prove useful in showing not how special humans are, but just how erroneous humankind's stubborn claim to superiority actually is. The 'rise of the machines' rhetoric, so often linked to dystopian views of cold, emotionless possibilities of human slavery at the hands of robots, offers more in the way of reorganising or re-thinking not just humanity and death alone, but the possibility of an entirely new species.

In *What is Philosophy?* (1994), Deleuze and Guattari argue that the purpose of art is to create what they call a 'people-to-come' (218), people who do not yet exist and who are characterised by 'non-thinking thought'. These people, according to Ronald Bogue, will dissolve 'conventional social categories and codes and invent new possibilities for life' (14).

Deleuze and Guattari were referring to something more metaphorical in this term, seeing the artist as producing work for a collective group that did not yet exist; they were not necessarily thinking of robots as a 'people-to-come'. But Deleuze and Guattari's concept is particularly fruitful when discussing the transition not only of humans, but of life. The invention of a people-to-come is enabled through the transformation of conventional notions of a collective group, in this case, humans. This is what makes popular culture so crucial in the transformation of a conventional understanding of being human. The artists behind *Blade Runner, Doctor Who* and *Westworld* imagine a people-to-come, people who are not defined and understood solely through biological essentialism. These people provide new ways of understanding what may constitute life in a post-human discourse, and what may, more importantly, constitute death in a non-biological sense.

The manner in which we have approached the earth and its beings has been a human-centred approach. The world and its phenomena have been reduced to a human view, outside of which we cannot comprehend, at least not easily. Human beings, too, have been programmed in this sense, by their own cultural world, and cannot easily accommodate the development of a robot species that can be seen to 'die'. Despite its evident implications, death has become an integral factor in determining and validating life, specifically, human life more so than animal, plant or inorganic life. Only that which lives is understood as being able to die, and only human death is seen to carry the greatest weight of significance, despite countless arguments to the contrary. This is due primarily to the value we have placed upon consciousness (at the expense of many other equally compelling factors).

But as I have shown in this book, the link between consciousness and human essentialism no longer remains entirely persuasive, meaning that life is not uniquely affiliated with consciousness, and that consciousness does not necessarily equate life. As Paul Ricoeur argued, notable philosophers such as Marx, Nietzsche and Freud sought to 'expose the illusions of consciousness and demot[e] its significance in the total economy of life' (Pearson and Large 2006: xviii). A machine, therefore, is something which can be understood as experiencing its own form of existence, including its own form of both life and death. Just as we can't imagine what it is to be a bat, in Thomas Nagel's view, we cannot imagine what it is to be a robot. But this inability to imagine such an existence, as Daniel Dennett has argued, does not remove the possibility of that being's existence. All it does, according to Dennett, is reveal our own inability to imagine what Deleuze sees as the 'people-to-come'. The problem, therefore, becomes one of a lack of imagination, an inability to imagine a robot species capable of living and dying, spurred by humanity's claim to superiority and their steadfast refusal to relinquish the biological essentialism that has so prejudiced other ways of living and dying. The notion of a conscious robot, therefore, becomes a necessary exercise in imagination.

In an effort to separate themselves from other animals, humans have erroneously claimed priority in the chain of life and existence. This is the reason why artificial intelligence has been met with such resistance in many cases, because of its radical implications for a species that may usurp humanity's position as the centre of all discourse and life. But this book has endeavoured to move away from the biological determinism that dictates much in the way of contemporary attitudes towards human behaviour and, more importantly, human essentialism and humanity's claim to superiority.

We can instead understand life and death as malleable concepts that can apply equally, if not more appropriately, to those beings that exhibit behaviour more befitting to humanity in a moral sense. For any claims relating to destruction at the hands of a machine neglect humanity's own destruction towards itself. Death therefore becomes a moral phenomenon, not a biological one.

If we maintain the link between death and biology, we risk undermining different ways of being and living. From this moment on, death may no longer be purely biological in scope; just as medical professionals have identified phenomena such as 'social death', so too may we develop an entirely new and radical way in which to approach machine death, as distinct from biological death but not necessarily less significant.

But life remains a biological concept for society, even when various kinds of 'life' are in the process of being changed or acknowledged, not only for humans, as is the case with Jahi McMath, but also in the case of machines, such as Pepper, the humanoid robot. Ironically, the increased fascination with the existence of potentially sentient robots once again puts humans at the centre of the equation. The robot throws us questions about what it ultimately means to be human but also, more importantly, asks us to think about ways of being *other* than human, of what may follow the human, of a being that retains the image or semblance of humanity but without the biological substrate (and presumably all the flaws therein). The robot is therefore a human that exists beyond biology.

Robots can never, in this way, be truly human in the biological sense; if the robot merely became human, mirroring to an exact replica both the psychological mannerisms and physical components of a human, then there would be no point in creating the robot, since it would simply repeat the image and actions of humanity. Instead, the robot seems destined to become what *Blade Runner* termed 'more human than human', reflecting certain traits of humanity while possessing its own unique characteristics. The robot, in this manner, serves to reflect an image of humanity itself, about its past and, more importantly, its uncertain future.

As humanity's lifespan continues to increase—with a number of humans dedicated to prolonging life to an indefinite extent—the presence of living machines does not merely serve to enlighten us to the possibility of different ways to be alive, but re-emphasises the importance of death in a time when mortality is in a state of flux. If anything, the presence of machine life reflects back to humanity the importance of our own mortality not in signifying our existence as humans, but in reinforcing the value of life itself as a temporary phenomenon. As a taken-for-granted phenomenon in the human world, death becomes a valuable indicator of life in the world of artificial consciousness.

REFERENCES

Deleuze, Gilles, and Guattari, Félix. *What Is Philosophy?* London: Verso, 1994.
Grayling, A.C. 'Culture Is What Separates Us from the Rest of the Living World'. *New Statesman.* May 8, 2013. Retrieved January 23, 2018, from https://www.newstatesman.com/culture/culture/2013/05/culture-what-separates-us-rest-living-world.
Pearson, Keith Ansell, and Large, Duncan. *The Nietzsche Reader.* Malden, Oxford, and Carlton: Blackwell, 2006.

BIBLIOGRAPHY

Adorno, Theodor, and Horkheimer, Max. *Dialectic of Enlightenment: Philosophical Fragments*. Stanford: Stanford University Press, 2002.

Anders, Charlie Jane, and Krell, Jason. '10 Robot Deaths That Were More Moving Than Almost Any Human's'. *Gizmodo*. December 6, 2013. Retrieved November 13, 2017, from https://io9.gizmodo.com/10-robot-deaths-that-were-more-moving-than-almost-any-h-1477252355.

Andress, Justin. 'What Happens to the Doctor When He Regenerates?' *Inverse*. April 20, 2016. Retrieved November 13, 2017, from https://www.inverse.com/article/14571-what-exactly-happens-to-the-doctor-when-he-regenerates.

Arendt, Hannah. *The Human Condition*. Chicago: University of Chicago Press, 1998.

Aristotle. *The Nicomachean Ethics of Aristotle*. London: Longmans, 1869.

Asaro, Peter. 'On Banning Autonomous Weapon Systems: Human Rights, Automation, and the Dehumanization of Lethal Decision-Making'. *International Review of the Red Cross*. Vol. 94, No. 886, 2012, pp. 687–709.

Aviv, Rachel. 'What Does It Mean to Die?' *The New Yorker*. February 5, 2018. Retrieved February 8, 2018, from https://www.newyorker.com/magazine/2018/02/05/what-does-it-mean-to-die.

Bar-Cohen, Yoseph, and Hanson, David. *The Coming Robot Revolution: Expectations and Fears About Emerging Intelligent, Humanlike Machines*. New York: Springer, 2009.

Becker, Ernest. *The Denial of Death*. New York: The Free Press, 1973.

© The Editor(s) (if applicable) and The Author(s) 2018
S. Lyons, *Death and the Machine*,
https://doi.org/10.1007/978-981-13-0335-7

Beijnon, Bjorn. 'Consciousness Without Bodies: Rethinking the Power of the Visualised Brain'. *World Futures: The Journal of New Paradigm Research.* Vol. 73, No. 2, 2017, pp. 78–88.

Berry, Christopher J. *Human Nature.* London: Macmillan, 1986.

Bloomfield, Masse. *Mankind in Transition: A View of the Distant Past, the Present and the Far Future.* Canoga Park: Masefield Books, 1993.

Borgstrom, Erica. 'Social Death'. *QJM: An International Journal of Medicine.* Vol. 110, No. 1, 2017, pp. 5–7.

Bricis, Larissa. 'A Philosopher Predicts How and When Robots Will Destroy Humanity'. *Techly.* September 25, 2017. Retrieved October 11, 2017, from https://www.techly.com.au/2017/09/22/philosopher-predicts-robots-will-destroy-humanity/.

Brodbeck, Luzius, Hauser, Simon, and Iida, Fumiya. 'Morphological Evolution of Physical Robots Through Model-Free Phenotype Development'. *PLoS One.* Vol. 10, No. 6, 2015.

Canton, James. *Future Smart: Managing the Game-Changing Trends That Will Transform Your World.* Boston: Da Capo Press, 2015.

Carroll, Michael. 'Part Human, Part Machine, Cyborgs Are Becoming a Reality'. *Newsweek.* July 31, 2014. Retrieved September 25, 2017, from http://www.newsweek.com/2014/08/08/cyborgs-are-walking-among-us-262132.html.

Charlton, Andrew, and Chalmers, Jim. 'The Robot Race: What does automation mean for the future of jobs?' The Monthly. November 2017. Retrieved January 12, 2018, from https://www.themonthly.com.au/issue/2017/november/1509454800/andrew-charlton-and-jim-chalmers/robot-race.

Clarke, Roger. '"Asimov's Laws of Robotics: Implications for Information Technology, Part 2." Institute of Electrical and Electronics Engineers'. *Computer.* Vol. 27, No. 1, 1994, pp. 57–65.

Colebrook, Claire. *Death of the Post Human: Essays on Extinction, Volume 1.* Ann Arbor: Open Humanities Press, 2014.

Cooter, Roger. 'The Dead Body'. *Companion to Medicine in the Twentieth Century.* Cooter, Roger and Pickstone, John (eds.). London and New York: Routledge, 2003, pp. 469–486.

Cozzolino, Philip J., and Blackie, Laura E. 'I Die, Therefore I Am: The Pursuit of Meaning in the Light of Death'. *The Experience of Meaning in Life: Classical Perspectives, Emerging Themes, and Controversies.* Hicks, Joshua A. (ed.). Netherlands: Springer, 2013, pp. 31–45.

Critchley, Simon. 'Being and Time Part 6: Death'. *The Guardian.* July 13, 2009. Retrieved September 25, 2017, from https://www.theguardian.com/commentisfree/belief/2009/jul/13/heidegger-being-time.

Deleuze, Gilles, and Guattari, Félix. *What Is Philosophy?* London: Verso, 1994.

Deleuze, Gilles, and Guattari, Félix. *Anti-oedipus: Capitalism and Schizophrenia.* London and New York: Continuum, 2004.

Dennett, Daniel. *Consciousness Explained*. London: Penguin, 1993.

Dennett, Daniel. *Brainchildren: Essays on Designing Minds*. Cambridge: The MIT Press, 1998.

Ebong, Maurice, and Bassey, Bassey J. *Environmental Perception and Human Behaviour*. Mushin: Macmillan Nigeria Publishers, 1995.

Eldredge, Niles, and Tattersall, Ian. *The Myths of Human Evolution*. New York: Columbia University Press, 1982.

Fedorov, Nikolai. *What Was Man Created For?: The Philosophy of the Common Task*. London: Honeyglen, 2008.

Fischer, John Martin. *The Metaphysics of Death*. Stanford: Stanford University Press, 1993.

Freud, Sigmund. *The Standard Edition of the Complete Psychological Works of Sigmund Freud: Volume XIV (1914–1916) On the History of the Psychoanalytic Movement, Papers on Metapsychology and Other Works*. London: Vintage, 2001.

Fuentes, Agustín, and Visala, Aku. *Conversations on Human Nature*. London and New York: Routledge, 2016.

Ghosh, Amitav. *The Great Derangement: Climate Change and the Unthinkable*. Chicago and London: The Chicago University Press, 2016.

Goldman, David. *How Civilizations Die: (And Why Islam Is Dying Too)*. Washington: Regnery, 2011.

Grayling, A.C. 'Culture Is What Separates Us from the Rest of the Living World'. *New Statesman*. May 8, 2013. Retrieved January 23, 2018, from https://www.newstatesman.com/culture/culture/2013/05/culture-what-separates-us-rest-living-world.

Griffin, Andrew. 'Humans Will Become Hybrids by 2030, Says Leading Google Engineer, with Tiny Robots Scurrying Around Our Brain to Help Us Think'. *The Independent*. June 4, 2015. Retrieved September 15, 2017, from http://www.independent.co.uk/life-style/gadgets-and-tech/news/humans-will-become-hybrids-by-2030-says-leading-google-engineer-with-tiny-robots-scurrying-around-10296200.html.

Hand, Michael. 'Regeneration and Resurrection'. *Doctor Who and Philosophy: Bigger on the Inside*. Lewis, Courtland and Smithka, Paula (eds.). Chicago and La Salle: Popular Culture and Philosophy, Open Court, 2011, pp. 213–224.

Haraway, Donna. 'A Cyborg Manifesto: Science, Technology, and Socialist Feminism in the Late Twentieth Century'. *Simians, Cyborgs and Women: The Reinvention of Nature*. New York: Routledge, 1991, pp. 149–181.

Heidegger, Martin. *On the Way to Language*. New York: Harper and Row, 1982.

Heidegger, Martin. *Being and Time*. Albany: New York Press, 2010.

Horowitz, Michael C. 'The Ethics and Morality of Robotic Warfare: Assessing The Debate Over Autonomous Weapons'. *Daedalus*. Vol. 145, No. 4, 2016, pp. 25–36.

Howarth, Glennys, and Leamon, Oliver. *Encyclopaedia of Death and Dying.* London and New York: Routledge, 2001.

Indick, William. *Movies and the Mind: Theories of the Great Psychoanalysts Applied to Film.* Jefferson: McFarland and Company, 2004.

Jacobs, Joseph. 'The Dying of Death'. *Fortnightly Review.* New Series 72, 1899, pp. 264–269.

Joy, Bill. 'Why the Future Doesn't Need Us'. *Wired.* April 1, 2000. Retrieved January 25, 2018, from https://www.wired.com/2000/04/joy-2/.

Keane, Daniel. 'Philosopher David Chalmers on Consciousness, the Hard Problem and the Nature of Reality'. *ABC News.* July 7, 2017. Retrieved November 11, 2017, from http://www.abc.net.au/news/2017-07-07/david-chalmers-and-the-puzzle-of-consciousness/8679884.

Koch, Christof. 'When Does Consciousness Arise in Human Babies?' *Scientific American.* September 1, 2009. Retrieved October 7, 2017, from https://www.scientificamerican.com/article/when-does-consciousness-arise/.

Koch, Christof, and Tononi, Giulio. 'Can Machines Be Conscious'. *IEEE Spectrum.* June 1, 2008. Retrieved October 9, 2017, from https://spectrum.ieee.org/biomedical/imaging/can-machines-be-conscious.

Kolbert, Elizabeth. *The Sixth Extinction: An Unnatural History.* New York: Henry Holt and Company, 2014.

Lagercrantz, Hugo, and Changeux, Jean-Pierre. 'The Emergence of Human Consciousness: From Fetal to Neonatal Life'. *Paediatric Research.* Vol. 65, 2009, pp. 255–260.

Larsen, Kristine. 'Everything Dies: The Message of Mortality in the Eccleston and Tennant Years'. *Doctor Who in Time and Space: Essays on Themes, Characters, History and Fandom, 1963–2012.* Leitch, Gillian I. (ed.). Jefferson: McFarland and Company, 2013, pp. 157–174.

Lukashevich, Stephen. *N. F. Fedorov (1828–1903): A Study in Russian Eupsychian and Utopian Thought.* Newark and London: University of Delaware Press, Associated University Presses, 1977.

McCauley, Lee. 'The Frankenstein Complex and Asimov's Three Laws', Association for the Advancement of Artificial Intelligence, 2007. Retrieved November 12, 2017, from https://www.aaai.org/Papers/Workshops/2007/WS-07-07/WS07-07-003.pdf.

Mori, Masahiro. *The Buddha in the Robot.* Tokyo: Kōsei Publishing, 1981.

Morton, Timothy. *Humankind: Solidarity with Nonhuman People.* London: Verso, 2017.

Nagel, Thomas. 'What Is It to Be a Bat?' *The Philosophical Review.* Vol. 83, No. 4, October 1974, pp. 435–450.

Nietzsche, Friedrich. *On the Genealogy of Morals and Ecce Homo.* New York: Vintage Books, 1989a.

Nietzsche, Friedrich. *Beyond Good and Evil: Prelude to a Philosophy of the Future.* New York: Vintage Books, 1989b.

Nussbaum, Martha. *Love's Knowledge: Essays on Philosophy and Literature*. New York: Oxford University Press, 1992.

Parisi, Domenico. *Future Robots: Towards a Robotic Science of Human Beings*. Advances in Interaction Studies. Volume 7. Amsterdam and Philadelphia: John Benjamins Publishing Company, 2014.

Pearson, Keith Ansell, and Large, Duncan. *The Nietzsche Reader*. Malden, Oxford, and Carlton: Blackwell, 2006.

Prioreschi, Plinio. *A History of Human Responses to Death: Mythologies, Rituals, and Ethics*. Studies in Health and Human Services. Volume 17. Lewiston: The Edwin Mellen Press, 1990.

Regalado, Antonio. 'What It Will Take for Computers to Be Conscious'. *MIT Technology Review*. October 2, 2014. Retrieved November 12, 2018, from https://www.technologyreview.com/s/531146/what-it-will-take-for-computers-to-be-conscious/.

Reichardt, Jasia. *Robots: Fact, Fiction and Prediction*. London: Thames and Hudson, 1978.

Rose, Steve. '"I've Seen Things You People Wouldn't Believe": What Blade Runner 2049's Dystopia Tells Us About 2017'. *The Guardian*. October 6, 2017. Retrieved October 12, 2017, from https://www.theguardian.com/film/2017/oct/06/blade-runner-2049-dystopian-vision-seen-things-wouldnt-believe.

Rowlands, Mark. *The Philosopher at the End of the Universe: Philosophy Explained Through Science Fiction Films*. London: Ebury Press, 2005.

Sammon, Paul M. *Future Noir: The Making of Blade Runner*. New York: Harper Paperbacks, 1996.

Scranton. Roy. *Learning to Die in the Anthropocene: Reflections on the End of a Civilisation*. San Francisco: City Lights Publishers, 2015.

Searle, John. 'Consciousness'. *Annual Review of Neuroscience*. Vol. 23, 2000, pp. 557–578.

Shewmon, D. Alan, and Shewmon, Elisabeth Seitz. 'The Semiotics of Death and Its Medical Implications'. *Brain Death and Disorders of Consciousness*. Machado, Calixto and Shewmon, D. Alan (eds.). Advances in Experimental Medicine and Biology. Vol. 550, 2004, pp. 89–114.

Sloman, Aaron. 'Why Asimov's Three Laws of Robotics Are Unethical'. 2006. Retrieved October 30, 2017, from http://www.cs.bham.ac.uk/research/projects/cogaff/misc/asimov-three-laws.html.

Tomasini, Floris. *Remembering and Disremembering the Dead: Posthumous Punishment, Harm and Redemption Over Time*. New York: Palgrave Macmillan, 2017.

Treder, Mike. 'Emancipation from Death'. *The Scientific Conquest of Death: Essays on Infinite Lifespans*. The Immortality Institute, 2004, pp. 187–196.

Tucker, Ian. 'Genevieve Bell: "Humanity's Greatest Fear Is About Being Irrelevant"'. *The Guardian*. November 27, 2016. Retrieved September 24, 2017, from https://www.theguardian.com/technology/2016/nov/27/genevieve-bell-ai-robotics-anthropologist-robots.

Turkle, Sherry. *Life on the Screen: Identity in the Age of the Internet.* New York: Simon and Schuster, 1995.

Vyverberg, Henry. *Human Nature, Cultural Diversity, and the French Enlightenment.* New York and Oxford: Oxford University Press, 1989.

Warren, Hannah. 'Should We Be Fighting Robots—Or Becoming Them?' *Techly.* August 23, 2016. Retrieved November 12, 2017, from https://www.techly.com.au/2016/08/23/fighting-robots-becoming/.

Yeung, Virginia. 'Mortality and Memory in Kazuo Ishiguro's *Never Let Me Go*'. *Transnational Literature.* Vol. 9, No. 2, May 2017, pp. 1–13.

Website

University of Cambridge. 'On the Origin of (Robot) Species', Research, 2015. Retrieved December 13, 2017, from http://www.cam.ac.uk/research/news/on-the-origin-of-robot-species.

INDEX

© The Editor(s) (if applicable) and The Author(s) 2018
S. Lyons, *Death and the Machine*,
https://doi.org/10.1007/978-981-13-0335-7

Printed by Printforce, the Netherlands